Signs of
my Times

Signs of
my Times

A life with deaf people

Martin Smith

BEECROFT PUBLICATIONS

2018

Signs of my Times
Copyright © Martin Smith 2018

Published in 2018 by
Beecroft Publications
72 Waterloo Lane, Bramley
Leeds LS13 2JF
www.beecroftpublications.co.uk

A CIP catalogue record for this book is available from the
British Library.

ISBN 978-0-9930909-5-0

Design and typography by Elizabeth Bee (c) 2018
Cover design by Ideas That Work, 31 Well Lane LS7 4PQ

Printed and bound in the Great Britain by
4edge Ltd, Essex

*My brother Lawrence read and corrected
the facts in the first chapter relating to events
before and just after my birth.
He hoped to read the rest of the book
but sadly died before publication.
I hope he would have been pleased with result.
To him and all my family I dedicate this book.*

Aged about 7

It was in desperation that my mother entered me for a poetry reading competition. I could speak well, learn poetry and recognise music, but at the age of eight there were very few other signs of intelligence. I stood on the platform and acted out, with appropriate rhythmic hand movements, the poem *Silver* by Walter De La Mare. There was much clapping, but to no avail – I was unplaced in the competition.

Contents

Illustrations

Photo credits:

Thanks go to Leeds Society for Deaf and Blind People for many of the photographs. The Oldham Society photograph on page 67 is © Alexander P Kapp (cc-by-sa/2.0). Those on pages 101 and 139 are reproduced with the kind permission of the Yorkshire Post. Every effort has been made to trace the owners of copyright material to obtain permission for its use. Where this has not been possible, appropriate acknowledgement and arrangements will be made for this to be corrected.

Preface

Every time I sign that time becomes mine
Gone are the slippery objects called words
The anxiety of meaning and spelling morphed
to an exciting existential freedom.
I am spaced by this implosion of sensory experience
The performance engages my whole being
It gives substance to life beyond expectation
Naked behavior verses a sanitised world.
I love it, this rich show
I can ingest, enjoy and believe in it
I am informed, I am a performer, I am connected.

The essence of this poem, if it can be called that, gives an insight into my experience of signing – of communication without words, using the language of deaf people. Deafness is a description of a state of being: it defines a group of people who share a perception of the world that comes from what they see and how they feel movement around them, and is a description used most commonly for people who are deaf at birth or in very early childhood. Deafness here defines a cultural, social and linguistic group, and is often signified by the use of a capital 'D'.

(That convention has been abandoned for this memoir to aid ease of reading.)

Some of the material in this book appeared in 2011 as *The Vanishing Missioner* – a first effort to tell my story of a hearing life in the deaf world, about attitudes towards education and social management that were deeply flawed, and also to record the history and evolution of the deaf community in Leeds.

Now, sixty years after I stumbled into a culture full of anomaly, I felt I should explain more about my actions and obsessions in trying to eradicate such attitudes in favour of great humanity and equity.

The process was bewildering for many, especially those who had, over generations, accepted the established, comfortable and unchallenging ways. It was also long, complex and intense, affecting many, including my own family. I would, I think, come to the same decisions now, except one: I would care more for my wife, my children and grandchildren. I hope you agree.

Acknowledgements

My first thanks must go to my wife Jill for fifty-five years of support, under sometimes trying circumstances. My family have always been supportive and interested.

Elizabeth Bee has been a revelation as to how an editor works and the book could never have been written without her. Thanks also to Michael Meadowcroft who gave me the title and to Adam Christie for the professional editing – creating a smooth text from my rough edges.

My next door neighbours, the Muries, have been a lifeline as they always helped with the technical support when I got stuck. Also, Dr Maurice Pearton and Marlene Godfrey who gave clear and honest opinions of my first book on the same subject.

Finally, thanks go to Evindra Lorenzo and the others who kept pushing me to complete this book and to Sarah Bown, of Wolverhampton University, who has been a caring source of knowledge.

1

The Childhood Mangle

THIS IS A TALE OF hindsight, of looking back and thinking about life – or rather about two lives, my personal life and the life of organisations around me; the personal and the collective. This process of recollection, of writing a memoir, brought together the clash of the consequences of my 'formative years' – and the attitudes I acquired as a middle-class white male born in 1937 – with nearly three-quarters of a century of accelerating social change. Driven by events, some were almost immediate and very logical (when we went to war, for example) while others that were less obvious and more deeply rooted in the social attitudes of the time have evolved more slowly and painfully. This is therefore a narrative about me versus the world – so the best way into that story is through me, my earliest experiences of that battle and the years before I found myself, ill-prepared and ill-equipped, facing challenges that have lasted my entire life.

War affected me from about the time of my earliest memories – probably amplified because I was in a country that had gone from depression to all-out conflict within ten years.

I was one in 1938 when my father, wanting to safeguard his wife and three young children, moved us to Devon from the family home in the Forest Hill suburb of south east London where I was born. The house had been paid for by my maternal grandfather who managed estates in Kent and Scotland for Lord Cornwallis.

My father, an architect, surveyor and structural engineer, had been invited to Germany in 1936 because of his knowledge of vibration. Amongst others, he worked for the Krupp armaments company and so was well aware of the looming conflict and the bombing which might ensue as part of Germany's military strategy. Highly qualified and talented, he was a charismatic individual who was away for most of my early life. During the war he served as the director of passive and active defence for the Ministry of Aircraft Production, established by prime minister Winston Churchill to overcome the supply problems facing the RAF during the Battle of Britain in 1940. The work involved finding space and facilities for the manufacture of Spitfire aircraft.

Our first refuge was a wooden bungalow in the strip village of Longdown, about three miles from Exeter. I well remember the water butt at the back. When I was two, I climbed onto it, fell in and stayed – half-submerged – until I was rescued by my brother Lawrence (Larry) and sister Olwen (Ommie); a fine game of hide-and-sink was a portent of calamities to come.

Such mishaps, which filled my early life and brought nothing but deep concern to family and friends, might today be considered self-harm or at least something requiring investigation. With childhood innocence, I would fire an arrow into the air, then watch mesmerised as it fell back towards earth, remaining motionless as it hit my forehead. Rather than the pain, I remember the sight of my toes hanging from my left foot after a seven-pound axe fell onto my foot. Mr Chandler, the local consultant surgeon and family friend, sewed them back. I fell from a tree and snapped my left wrist in two, leaving the bone sticking out through the skin. Holding onto my limp arm I cried 'it's my bowling arm' when my mother appeared. I had not been at the local junior school long when the vicar of nearby Clyst St Mary ran me over with his car. That accident dented a wheel cover and cut my head; the scar is still visible. The blood in the road from the accident was a source of morbid interest to fellow pupils.

Desperate to please, I volunteered for anything and everything. Attached to a rope, I tested the ice before Larry and his friends skated on a frozen pond, going home soaked several times. I ran up and down a field so they could fire air guns at a moving target. I crouched inside an iron container in a disused quarry so they could hurl stones. I quickly became a regular and well-known patient at the Royal Devon and Exeter Hospital accident and emergency department.

Both Larry and Olwen were horsey. They rode our pony, Tinkerbell, through the house and would take part in gymkhanas

Larry, me and Olwen on ice, winter 1947

3

and similar events. (Larry became an accomplished point-to-pointer and I remember the excitement of his daring and skilled horsemanship.) Once, I even tried to blow 'gone away' on a hunting horn as he and Olwen rode with the local hounds.

My sister Olwen was two years younger than Larry, four years older than me and the brightest of the three of us. My father however strongly believed that women existed to do his bidding, so Olwen had to cope with his domineering. My mother appeared to comply, seemingly slaving away to meet his every need. She would sit, curled up beside a big fireplace, reading copiously as she waited for a call that my father was on his way from London. However she maintained another, separate, life of which he knew little if anything. She loved guiding and founded the Devon branch of the Trefoil Guild (for adult guides) as well as being an active member of the Women's Royal Voluntary Service. She won a following as an after-dinner speaker. I know she spoke at the Salmon Supper in Topsham, an annual celebration of the wild fish caught on the River Exe, but not what she talked about, be that the WRVS or her much-loved Trefoil Guild. I do know though that my father never heard her.

Our family was Anglican and formal. We went to church regularly and, by nine, I'd learned to toll the five-minute bell, summoning the villagers to prayer at the ancient church of St John the Baptist at Holcombe Burnell, half-a-mile from Longdown and four miles west of Exeter. The original intimate church was Norman but had been largely rebuilt in the 1840s. The vicar, Christopher Poulton, was kind and caring. After my maternal grandmother left London, following our departure, he and his wife cared for her at the large white vicarage, with its views of Topsham, Exeter and the sea in one direction and Dartmoor in the other.

In 1940, we moved towards the heart of Longdown, making a home in a large bungalow called St Margaret's, set in an acre of grounds, with a delightful view over a deep valley; the surrounding woods and fields became my personal playground. St Margaret's remained my much-loved home for many years and my roots remain in those rural communities.

Our home,
St Margaret's

My parents expected much of their children. My brother and sister were privately educated. Larry went first to Ide School and then, in 1940, to Exeter School while a tutor 'prepared' Olwen for the city's Maynard School for Girls. As a five-year-old, my education began at Holcombe Burnell village school. I walked the two miles each way, carrying my sandwiches and, I think, a halfpenny a day for milk in the morning. Today, safety fears deny children such independence, but, in 1942, rural traffic was never very busy. Near the church and a large house called The Barton, the single-roomed school building – with toilets round the back – housed about twenty children, aged between five and fourteen, in a single large class. This was my first taste of a different community, a different language and a different behaviour from those demanded at home. The pupils were like a gang. We roamed around together after school. I watched as foxes, caught in snares, were stoned to death and birds' nests were destroyed by catapults. We fought with children from other villages and had games that involved urinating in the woods. We bonded with the 'I'll show you mine if you show me yours' dares typical of those ages.

I also learned that how one sounded could be important. The distinctly Devonian tones of the classroom contrasted greatly with pronunciation at home. The first BBC director general, (Lord) John Reith was a role model, so middle-class speech and behaviour were obligatory. My father definitely did not want a 'yokel' son, so I adopted two ways of speaking, slipping easily from one to the other according to the company. (Now, with sign language, I have a third.)

My progress at school was negligible so my parents arranged for extra, private, English tuition from Nellie Kendal, a wonderful, cultured older lady who had been an early member of the English Folk Dance and Song Society. She lived in a small cottage, high above the village, where I was enchanted by folk songs collected by Cecil Sharp and Ralph Vaughan Williams. I also enjoyed the physical exercise of helping her by pumping water from her garden well. During my time with Nellie Kendal my sensitivity towards words and music grew, at the expense of formal learning. I discovered an accurate singing voice and a memory for music. I may have inherited this – and my interest in sport – from my paternal grandfather, a schoolmaster. His voice was good enough to win him an invitation to join the young D'Oyly Carte opera company, which my grandmother quickly repressed. (He played rugby for Gloucester too.) When my father noticed my ability he had me learn songs by Mozart and Wagner, so I could sing to him in our music room on his visits from London.

My strong Devonian accent made me acceptable locally. I knew the villagers, spending holidays with two woodsmen from the nearby Perridge estate, Lance Tricky and Billy Stone (who was deaf). Every day, my mother packed me off for more adventures with my imaginary friend Hacks. He came everywhere with me and also needed feeding, so armed with two lots of sandwiches we'd make our way to the cottages where Mr Tricky and Mr Stone lived. These great friends showed me where the redstarts nested and the orchids grew. I listened as water voles plopped into the Perridge pond and speckled wood butterflies spiralled in sun-filled glades. All of nature became a friend, particularly butterflies and moths. Once, my mother found more than seventy cabbage white caterpillars crawling all over me. I reared moths through every stage of their lives before releasing them and brought elephant hawk caterpillars back from a fourteen-mile cycle ride along the Exe estuary to Dawlish Warren. Books I had been given nurtured my interest and, when my parents went away leaving their children behind, I'd stay with my father's boss, Mr BW Adkin, who had his own, huge collection of butterflies and moths.

War provided spectacles too. I remember watching Exeter and the cathedral ablaze after bombing, farms being strafed and seeing the rear gunners in low-flying planes waiting to open fire. A nearby farmer, Mr Isaacs, would stand in his field, blasting both barrels of his twelve-bore shotgun angrily into the sky while Tribble, our gardener, stood stock-still among the vegetables like a lump of Devonian beer stone.

Mr Tribble

7

I was eight when the war ended and duty no longer kept my father in London as much. I did not know him, but he assumed a powerful and controlling influence. He returned to the College of Estate Management in Knightsbridge, London (now part of the University of Reading) as director of building studies for a period, before setting up his own architectural practice with offices in London and Exeter, so he could spend more time in Devon. My world had to change to meet his. He involved the whole family in transforming the garden, which was big enough for a full-size cricket pitch. We even had a net. Each summer, rather than do my homework, I'd practise my bowling with Larry. Within a couple of years, I could hit the stumps with about one ball in six. I'd play with my father and brother, but mother warned me that bowling out my father was not a good idea. Cricket, and later rugby, filled my time. I also learned to swim and to sail, but the tennis court remained unappreciated until it became a way to meet girls.

Altogether, this was a magical world for a little boy, even one scared of a largely absentee father with very different expectations of learning and development. Although I had learned how to fit in socially, I still had no hope of academic growth at the village school. As a nine-year-old, I was removed and was sent to a smart private establishment – Miss Chalice's. The culture change was immense. Away went the contact with the village children and the rich local vocabulary. I quickly learned to use my 'home voice' to fit in with my middle-class contemporaries.

I made a lifelong friend there in Chris Webber. (Chris went on to a successful career in finance; we had been friends for nearly seventy years when he died.) Chris and I would pick fights with more genteel schoolmates, frequently provoking complaints from other parents. We bonded, becoming closer friends as our respective learning problems were recognised. He was dyslexic and I – as I found out much later – was 'cross lateral'. Being cross lateral needs some explanation as it shaped much of what has happened to me since those early mishaps: it is a state where neither side of a person's brain is dominant. Such people can be right-handed and left-footed or left-handed and right-footed. This, and dyslexia, can both affect learning. My reading skills were good, but my writing was extremely erratic – factors that shaped much of my life. Some days I could spell; others I could not. The consequent anxiety worsened after I broke my wrist and the bones locked after being set. In sport, having a cross laterality was an advantage; I was ambidextrous and could naturally hit and kick a ball with either hand or foot. I could dance well too.

When Chris and I moved from Miss Chalice's school to Exeter Preparatory School, we spent most of our time sharing the dubious honour of being bottom of the class. There, as anywhere in the 1940s, no one recognised 'learning disability'. However, although we were good at sport, not disruptive and our parents paid the fees, we took a long time to settle down. My prep school time remains a blur. I captained both the cricket and football teams but learned nothing academically. Chris and I were both older than our classmates, as we arrived after them, and life got worse when we were moved up a year to join our contemporaries. I never caught up, but sport – and having an elder brother already there – got me into the main school. Apart from sport, I was known for my interest in moths and butterflies, so both pupils and masters brought me specimens to identify including, once, two large copulating death's-head hawkmoths.

All I remember of class time at the main school is the anxiety, while longing for the mental freedom of sport that maintained me throughout those years. I continued to be almost a complete failure in the classroom but remember passing one exam – English literature – probably because the master, RW Bell, read Chaucer to us in old English. (Years later, I learned that he was so anxious about his spelling that he always kept a dictionary with him.) I played rugby and hockey for county public school teams and cricket for Exeter. My parents threw money at this too, paying for extra coaching at Lord's from professionals Jim Simms and Jack Robertson. To help, my mother gave me books about high adventure and daring deeds. Spencer Chapman's *The Jungle's Neutral* filled me with enthusiasm – but I didn't know what for.

School was a perpetual clash of daily classroom anxiety and extramural confidence – be that in sport, on the stage, in the choir or in pursuing girls. I may have been useless academically but intuitive abilities emerged. I could name nearly all the school's four hundred pupils, while music met an emotional need. I loved the sound and the harmony of singing; they made more sense than the words, even then. I played a drum in the cadet band and took a leading part in a production of Gilbert and Sullivan's *Trial by Jury*, about a broken marriage promise. My teenage interest in girls had become well-known, so some thought me typecast.

No one really thought about religion in the late 1940s and early 50s; it was assumed and passive. Chapel was an integral aspect of school and, as I enjoyed singing, I went each morning as a member of the choir. Even as my voice broke I could contribute to the sound in some way. It was a pleasant experience and softened the fear of approaching lessons. The chaplain was Christopher Poulton, who had moved to Exeter from our rural parish. He prepared me for my confirmation – at Crediton parish church. As I knelt in front of Bishop William Surtees, I was overcome with emotion and fainted. I was carried out and taken home, probably not ready for the commitment. I could easily be overtaken by my emotions but found some comfort in religion – I was later confirmed in Rev Poulton's parish in Exeter.

Accidents continued. I set fire to the kitchen (and myself) while frying. I backed a car into a rose arbour on the side of the house. I covered myself in concentrated nitric acid, so weakening my cadet uniform that it fell apart during a parade. I joined the RAF cadets and went to Lossiemouth air base – where I managed to open a parachute on the ground. There was a wind blowing and I had to be rescued as I was dragged across the runway. Expressing interest in an air force career, I was flown with five others in an Anson aircraft for a three-day assessment at RAF Hendon, in north London. At the final interview, I said I was aiming for the navy. I was ignominiously demoted from lance corporal to cadet. I did however keep my word, joining the Royal Naval Volunteer Reserve not long after that.

Many years later, my brother met one of his old school friends who asked him how I had got on in life. Surprised, my brother asked why he enquired. The friend said that he had understood that I was a little bit 'simple'.

By the time I was sixteen, I had sat fourteen O level exams, seven at a time, and passed only the one. I left school to go to a cramming college in London. Before I left, my maths teacher Jake Ledger, a Canadian, had said in a typically laconic drawl, 'Smith, don't accept any wooden money, 'cos it ain't worth a thing.' With this observation on my ability, my school career ended. Despite my lack of success, my father did not deny me the week away with him that was a family tradition on leaving school. While Larry went skiing in Switzerland and Olwen visited Iceland, I chose the Edinburgh festival. I saw Sir John Barbirolli conduct Mahler's ninth symphony in the Usher Hall and spent hours fascinated by the music, costume and dance in the Diaghilev exhibition.

The Borlands cramming college fulfilled its name. I had to concentrate, being allowed only one evening a week for cricket practice, despite playing for the club in Addiscombe at weekends. I missed rugby but played hockey dispassionately in the autumn; it did not fire my imagination. I worked at Borlands in the morning and then walked to the National Liberal Club near Charing Cross, where my father and brother were members, each afternoon to study in the Gladstone Library. Peters, the porter, kept me up-to-date with family news, so my middle-class existence was not threatened.

I lodged with Maurice Pearton, an Oxford graduate and an academic, who helped me greatly. His introduction to Lady Hamilton and her 'modelling' career brought so much life to history that I passed that O level with a mark of seventy per cent, having only got twenty-nine per cent at school. He provided me with fascinating insights into the lives of composers such as Erik Satie and Hugo Wolf, adding to my joy of Mahler who was already firmly established as a favourite. Maurice became my mentor and remains so today.

Passing English and geography (in addition to history), but failing maths and science (again) did a little to diminish the anxiety of learning that stayed with me for decades, so I returned to Exeter with minimal success – and four months to wait before starting national service. I found work as a temporary village postman while filling my leisure time with rugby and girls. I remember that summer well as it was when myxomatosis was killing thousands of rabbits. I tried to ease the painful deaths of as many as I could while pedalling to deliver letters to important local figures such as jet engine inventor Sir Frank Whittle at Culver and the Studholme family at Perridge House.

My national service call-up took me to the Royal Navy's Victoria barracks in Portsmouth, first used by the infantry but taken over by the Royal Navy after the Second World War. Years before, I had attempted the entrance exam for the Royal Naval College in Dartmouth, where officers were trained. I came ninth from bottom. By the time national service started, having already had some initial instruction while in the Reserve, I already knew how to march, salute and shoot. After some basic training I was selected to play cricket for Portsmouth United Services and the navy, while everyone else went off for further training. I was even rewarded with parental approbation when my father and mother came to see me turn out for a navy team at my old home ground in Exeter. At last, they could be pleased and proud.

After about a month, I caught up with the other five hundred conscripts on a ship bound for Bergen in Norway, itself an educational voyage. A Liverpudlian occupied the next hammock, wearing knuckle dusters while he slept. My Reserve experience helped me weather a gale, while most of my mess mates were sick. Ashore, I enjoyed visiting the home of composer Edvard Grieg and meeting contemporaries who entertained me – finding life a joy, away from pressure and competition.

Back at sea, I was one day assigned to clean the brasses outside the captain's cabin. I was surprised to hear a voice from inside ask if I was the Smith who played cricket. I said yes and the door opened. That commanding officer, Anthony Miers (later Sir Anthony), had been awarded the Distinguished Service Order and Victoria Cross for wartime service. A huge character, and totally committed to sport, he soon got me into civilian clothing to masquerade as a member of the officers' cricket team, even though I was just an ordinary seaman. 'Gamp' Miers, as he was known, seemed to appreciate that I was not afraid of social or physical situations. On the cricket field I once wilfully disobeyed him and he roared a challenge at me saying 'If I was not the captain of the ship and you were not the most junior ordinary seaman, Smith, I would challenge you to a duel'. When I asked if he wanted swords or pistols, he was highly amused.

Somehow, at the end of the short period of training, I was awarded the best entry prize – a Royal Navy whistle called a 'bosun's call'. I thought this wrong and openly passed the commendation to someone far more deserving, Roger Bamborough. This simultaneously caused consternation while being impressive enough to earn me an invitation to interview for a commission.

I faced the officer assessment back in Portsmouth. An attractive Wren – a member of the Women's Royal Naval Service (or WRNS) – carried out a psychological test and revealed a shared interest in Mahler. I passed the IQ test too and celebrated at Monks Bar in Old Portsmouth with the Wren. I found myself in the company of Roger Bamborough, back on board the aircraft carrier HMS *Theseus,* for officer training. There, my education anxieties again came to the fore. Eleven others on the course were either Oxbridge graduates or on their way to such academic prowess. Another was a qualified merchant navy second mate while I was the dunce fighting a losing battle with maths and celestial navigation. I failed, felt humiliated, but got a second chance. My salvation was an instructor officer determined that I should pass. My seamanship was fine and I could recite the rules of the sea almost verbatim, but my navigation and log-keeping were apparently among the worst ever seen. I did qualify, but ten months was the longest anyone had ever spent on the course. I changed from the bell bottoms of the ordinary seaman into a smart officer's uniform and set off for home. On the train from Plymouth to Exeter, I kept looking in the mirror: was this really me? Such success had never come to me before.

In midshipman's uniform, aged 19

The delay – and being the only person qualifying at that time – denied me a place on a passing out parade. Instead, I simply went from queuing for food to be slopped onto a tray in the lower deck mess to, a few days later, being served by stewards in the officers' wardroom.

My second, and final, year of national service included two trips to the Mediterranean, a skiing holiday and playing hockey for the Mediterranean fleet in Malta. I also made lasting friends, in particular, Anthony French who has stayed close ever since. One trip was not without incident. Olwen's husband, my brother-in-law, John St Aubyn Hartley, almost literally ran into me when a helicopter could not find his ship and dropped him on mine. He was carrying a parcel from my mother in Exeter, handed to him two days earlier. 'Give this to Martin when you see him,' she said. My ship was fifty miles off Malta! That year – 1956 – also provided me with my only real experience of war, when I was second in command of a ship's operations room during the Suez crisis.

Before national service, I had become a 'born again' Christian after following one girlfriend to a religious retreat at Leigh Abbey in north Devon. That provoked another emotional dilemma – fitting all life into a moral framework. I had been assigned to another aircraft carrier, HMS *Albion*, where I met a newly-commissioned midshipman who said he was a Christian, having trouble reconciling the navy's 'apartheid' between the officer class in the wardroom and the 'other ranks' on the lower decks. Despite talking a little, we never became friends. He had the strength of character to abandon his navy commission and enter the priesthood while I did not.

I remembered my transition to becoming an officer – and wondered whether the accompanying advantages indicated human superiority of some sort or just rewarded one for jumping through hoops to achieve academic success, thinking that more often than not background and privilege still then accompanied one another. I liked being called 'Sir', even if that came (sometimes) with fairly clear contempt. I did however find a way to deal with this. Standing in for a senior colleague for 'rounds' – to inspect the messes one evening – one welcomed me with laughter. I left them standing to attention while I went round the rest of the ship, leaving them unamused but gaining me respect.

I turned down the offer of a permanent commission when my national service came to an end in spring 1957, thinking civilian life would welcome me back. Demobbed, I was hopeful but my confidence was fragile. Peers respected my sporting abilities but little else. What, as a twenty-year-old, was I to do? I had an officer's accent, some culture but nothing on which to base a career. My few O levels were far from enough to get to university so the middle-class professional life expected to emanate from my family and upbringing was a forlorn hope. My only civilian work experience had been the few months as a postman and in the Exeter office of my father's business. Family influence got me one interview – for personnel work – which I again failed.

After a few months, I ended up at Exeter labour exchange in a dinner jacket, while my brother Larry, similarly dressed, waited outside in the blue soft-top family Daimler, ready to drive us to a cocktail party; characteristic of the incongruity that seems to have accompanied me through life. The employment officer showed me two possible jobs – one in an Exeter insurance office, the other as trainee welfare officer in the deaf and dumb department of the Leeds Incorporated Institution for the Blind, Deaf and Dumb. The job description said interests in sport and religion were essential. I had those and the job sounded right. I also wanted to leave home. Leeds was three hundred miles away and I had a girlfriend in West Hartlepool, which, my limited geography told me, was 'somewhere in the north', near Leeds, and certainly further up the map than the line between Bristol and Potters Bar. (We had met when I had been taken off my ship with suspected rubella and isolated in hospital in West Hartlepool. The infection turned out to be glandular fever. A visiting girl, seeing I was alone, decided to befriend me and subsequently became my girlfriend.)

I knew nothing about deaf people. All I could think of was, years earlier, seeing a crocodile of sad-looking children, in dark raincoats, holding on to the railings of Exeter's Victoria Park Road, while I was playing rugby. Someone told me they were from the deaf and dumb school in nearby St Leonard's. I had played rugby and cricket with one of the teachers there, John Stark, and he gave me a reference when I applied to work in Leeds.

I remember the interview in Leeds as intense, but having become more cunning and needy, I sat still, spoke properly and got the job. The paid trip from Exeter also meant I could see my girlfriend in Hartlepool, so I travelled on northwards. Much to my surprise, that journey took longer than I expected.

My father was so bewildered by my choice that he did not speak to me for eight months, while my mother was pleased but concerned. She bought me warm Wolsey underwear as protection from the northern cold and a subscription to the art magazine *Studio*, hoping I would retain some culture. (I suspect that neither Henry Moore or Barbara Hepworth had yet made their mark in Exeter.)

Life might, until then, have had some challenges but my privileged protected upbringing, insular and conservative, certainly hadn't prepared me for what was to come; the harsh realities of a controlled community.

Apart from going to prison or starting work in a foreign country, I cannot imagine anything more bewildering.

2

Northern Exposure

I'D ARRIVED IN A CITY those in the south called 'mucky', my search for some kind of a job now over. I even had somewhere to live – at the YMCA hostel in Chapel Allerton. I rode from the city centre on a very shaky tram, seeing Briggate, North Street, going past the public dispensary, along Chapeltown Road passed the main synagogue before emerging into the leafier environment of Harrogate Road. I got off at the police station and hauled my gear up Allerton Hill to be met by the hostel warden, a harassed looking man. He showed me to the room I'd be sharing with two others, Reg and Ebo – but not for long; a fire broke out on my second night there and we were all moved into university accommodation. Reg and Ebo came from conflicting parts of Nigeria but were great friends. I had never met black people before in the UK; Exeter was not a great pull for arrivals looking for work or attempting to integrate into British life. Black people were rare in Exeter's schools and streets as well as in the Royal Navy. The other hostel occupants were mainly sixteen-year-old lads. I was twenty and, after national service, considered myself to be grown up, so we didn't have much in common. Finding somewhere else to live took a few weeks.

Leeds was vibrant in 1957. Diverse industry, underpinned by the clothing trade, provided almost full employment. Burton's, Jackson the Tailors and the Fifty Shilling Tailors were among the better-known. The espresso coffee bars were well established. The show *Expresso Bongo* played at the Grand Theatre, before its London failure. Lewis Jones, a great rugby hero who ran as fast sideways as he did forward, played with the likes of Arthur Clues at Headingley and Yorkshire were strong at cricket. Ravi Shankar, George Melly and an outpost of Ronnie Scott's Jazz Club entertained, as did lunchtime concerts in the city museum on Park Row. Such richness was waiting to be explored, but work and its first challenges had to be faced.

I arrived at 135 Albion Street having no idea what to expect. I came 'Devon red and raw' into an organisation so long established that its concept of service had not changed since the early 1870s. I was naïvely impressionable and desperate to learn, earn and to please. This was my first full-time civilian job. I had no psychological props or experience to support me or allow me to compare the organisation against any others; instinctively I knew it would be different. I knew too that I had to help people who were deaf and dumb from the perspective of Christian endeavour but I had no skills; I was a cavalier without a sword. My way into this life was through the sombre entrance of the Leeds Incorporated Institution for the Blind and the Adult Deaf and Dumb; what a revealing name, I'll call it 'the organisation'.

My recollections of getting started that first week are best condensed into an anecdote from the war in Vietnam a decade later. I remember the story of an officer saying, after US troops had razed a settlement to the ground, 'We had to destroy the village in order to save it'. This still haunts me – as a permanent reminder of how any mission pursued with dogged zeal can defeat itself, choking its core passion.

Describing events fifty years ago may seem to risk accuracy, but the stark setting and sharp experiences give me confidence that my memory remains vivid. My mind had wandered so much on my way across Leeds that I could easily have tripped on the step as I went inside that Monday morning.

The entrance was positioned between two other businesses – a car dealership and a gun shop which rented space from the organisation. I approached a red neon sign, saying "Deaf", in capital letters. I walked up the two steps to the door, finding more stairs, swing doors and a dark hall inside. I couldn't remember much from my interview visit but now, 'for real', I noticed more. A huge mirror hung on the wall to the left. In front, steep stairs led to meeting rooms and other activity areas,  including a curtained off chapel, youth rooms for table tennis, three snooker tables, darts, dominoes and a small library full of old books, kindly given but seldom read. (By the mid-fifties, literacy skills amongst deaf people had plummeted and reading was not usual, as it had been at the turn of the century). Getting wheelchairs in was almost impossible. Ahead, a big blackboard listed each week's activities and any diktats the superintendent-missioner deemed important. This included jumble sales, harvest festivals and visiting preachers beside messages such as 'look what your superintendent has done for you' and reminders of

The Albion Street entrance

money raised for 'treats' such as holiday trips or Christmas gifts; the deaf recipients had to be duly grateful to the providers. I passed a man in a boilersuit. He said nothing. Later, I found out he was Mr Darville, the caretaker, and himself deaf.

On the left, another passage under the stairs led to a waiting room with old, tip-up seats from a disused cinema. Beyond that were the offices, reached through a glass-panelled door with a waist-high blocking door, lockable on the inside. I was shown the office of the trainee welfare officer, mine for the next four years. It was small with a mirror and a bookcase full of dusty old brown tomes, many about the bleak events of the First World War. On the desk, my boss had left a card showing the positions of the fingers and hands needed to produce a two-handed manual alphabet. I was left alone to learn this as a first task. I struggled, I was not to be a natural, either as a finger speller (of English) or in learning sign language.

I spent the rest of the day exploring the building and meeting the other staff. Jimmy Hudson was the boss, the missioner-superintendent. A small man, he was among the better-known characters on the national deaf scene, dominated at that time by the British Deaf and Dumb Society. Charismatic, with endless energy, he was totally driven in the care and protection of deaf people. With deaf parents, he had 'the badge' – of family experience and being acceptable to other deaf people. I was introduced to Jimmy's wife, Mary, and the (partially deaf) lady welfare officer. She was medically qualified and had been a fever nurse while Mary, who was equally driven and devoted, worked part-time in accounts and catering. I also met Joan Brocklesby, the organisation's general secretary. A no-nonsense spinster, she was passionately involved with Leeds Parish Church. She conducted and played the piano for the Leeds Blind Choir and organised the braille library in the Blind Institute and Workshops on Roundhay Road, and became a kind and thoughtful support for me. (She delighted those who loved her when she married.) Together, the organisation's few staff all seemed totally secure and competent; I felt exactly the opposite.

Work the next day started with a staff meeting at 9.30am. This seemed to be about general health and welfare as illness and hospitalisation were discussed. I quickly learned that the lady welfare officer had to visit all the city's deaf people regularly so she could report on their welfare and activities. When I was introduced to one dignified old man, I fumbled as I tried to communicate. He said something I could not understand. I asked what it was and was told 'stupid welfare can't spell'. Such directness quickly became familiar; he didn't know I couldn't spell anyway. Later, two Jewish looking women – sisters-in-law Brina and Yetta Custin – appeared outside the office. I tried to talk to them. Great, I thought, they had speech, especially Yetta, and I showed them pictures of my family. Quickly, my boss told me not to be so familiar.

Every morning, the library/reading room quickly filled with older men, mainly in their seventies, keen to get to the newspapers. Some could read, as they'd been to school fifty years earlier. I took a while to realise that their interests were quite focused; they saw the room as an annexe to a nearby betting shop.

In the afternoon I was introduced to the old people's group. When I walked into the biggest room, about twenty people were waiting. They had been warned of my first appearance but I couldn't even say good afternoon in sign language then, so I just stood in front of them, nodding and smiling. I was, it transpired, required to contribute to weekly 'Darby and Joan' activities; blind whist one week, bingo the next. I became the caller when I could count on my hands. I was bewildered. The culture, language and context were all unknown. I also had to learn how to make sandwiches – fish paste one week, meat paste the following week – and to lay them out symmetrically. The missioner's wife baked buns at home – as my wife Jill had to do years later – and a volunteer lady in a hat poured the tea. The clients had a rota for washing up; a 'non-executive' function.

After that, I got an hour to eat. The break was a relief but I had no one to talk to. Coming back at 6.30pm, I ran into the, for me, strange sounds of deaf people. These were bizarre, coming from people who could not hear themselves, and unlike any other noises I had ever heard. They had no accent or rhythm and I could not tell if they came from men or women; it was a real cacophony. It took me years to discover who created which sounds. (Eventually, when I could audibly identify each person, the strangeness receded, as did the unease.) I remember walking round the building that evening, feeling deeply detached as I watched billiards, snooker, darts, dominoes and table tennis all being played with great intensity. Some had brought their children, who ran round the spiral staircases. I was sent to control them, so their parents could play bingo in peace. Such activities

Snooker tables in
the games room

had been recorded as happening, unchanged for decades, by Nick Waite in *Alone in A Silent World,* his 2016 history of the community in South Yorkshire. Nothing seemed to have changed.

I also found about twenty people waiting outside the office for the missioner. They'd come with various needs – from booking interpreters for hospital and other appointments, filling in tax forms, writing hospital letters, dealing with job difficulties, family and community disputes, legal matters, loans and many other perceived problems. The range seemed unlimited. Tradition said the missioner knew best and could solve every care and worry. There was always a queue. I was far too junior to provide such support. Even two or three years into the job few people came to me. Over time, I became increasingly convinced that this approach encouraged dependency rather than independence.

As the building did not 'belong' to deaf people they could take no responsibility for its care or management, so, at 10pm, I had to clear the premises and, with Mr Darville the caretaker, lock up. My first experience of deaf culture had been raucous, direct, frightening and challenging.

Going home, I saw a crowd of deaf people under the street lights continuing their conversations. I carefully avoided contact; I was now back in my different world. Getting off the tram in Chapel Allerton I went into a coffee bar on the corner of Harrogate Road and West Hill Terrace. Although about to close, I was served and the owners talked to me, providing the respite I wanted. I quickly became a regular and often helped clean up, mopping the floors at closing time, a skill I had acquired in the navy. Being with hearing peers, carrying out a familiar task, felt normal.

Wednesdays were devoted to the deafblind. Leeds Welfare Services, who also provided hot lunches, brought about fifteen people from their homes. They were special as this was considered the worst condition, but to be fully deserving they had to be totally blind and totally deaf. Being deaf from before they could develop speech demanded special communication skills and often language modifications too. A group of carers talked to them using the deafblind manual alphabet. The carers seemed severe but very competent communicators. I also had to learn this system of spelling letters on someone's hand. When they were introduced, I was not sure what to do but tried to make contact. I was never comfortable among the deafblind although I did make friends with two people who could speak and had gone both blind and partially deaf later in life. The issues surrounding deafblind people were, and are, too demanding for me. I could never bring myself to barge in and out of their lives. I still don't know what anyone can do to improve their lives without being totally committed to them.

Thursday was the hard-of-hearing day, when those in the Leeds and District Hard of Hearing Club gathered. These people were treated very differently from the deafblind. They were less important as they were 'normal' people who had lost some hearing. Perhaps unsurprisingly, they had little status in the hierarchy of the organisation's client groups. Later, I learned about their needs but only, fifty years later, when my own hearing and sight began failing did I appreciate just how many adjustments are needed. Consequently, Thursday became my regular day off for the next four years. I had time to form a non-deaf life in Leeds. Having thought, in typical southern ignorance, that the north was full of muck, brass and little culture I had lots to learn. Luckily, one lunchtime that first week I saw an Exeter girl, Gloria Keane, walking up the Headrow, Leeds' main thoroughfare. Her family moved when her father was promoted to manage a new Marks and Spencer's branch. She and her friend Tricia Johnston invited me for coffee, providing my entry to the café society of the time, a great mix of traditional Yorkshire folk and, particularly, young Jewish professionals. I wasn't lonely for long. I made friends easily with people in cafés and coffee bars, but not pubs; alcohol was out of bounds for a trainee missioner – and beyond my means.

Early Thursdays were spent visiting agents and flat hunting before a pattern developed, of rest, study and socialising. Like every twenty-year-old, learning how to survive was essential. Such time became precious. I had one weekend off each month. For the first six, I travelled to West Hartlepool to be with the girl who had prompted my move north. She sensibly ended the relationship when she realised I had no space for anything serious in a world mentally cramped by such amazing new work experiences.

On my first Friday, I was sent to visit the huge High Royds psychiatric institution at Menston outside Leeds. I had to report on the conditions of four deaf people. I had no idea why they were there. I knew nothing about their mental state in advance and I had never been inside such a place, but I did have suitable gifts – cigarettes and chocolate. Getting off the blue Samuel Ledgard bus at White Cross, I walked up the long winding drive to the main entrance. The building was massive, imposing and I had never seen anything like it, except perhaps

High Royds, Menston

Dartmoor prison in the mist. I was told there were more than two thousand patients there. The corridors seemed endless. I apprehensively walked past patients sitting, leaning against the walls with their legs stretched out before reaching a locked pen where people with epilepsy were endlessly singing:

'Buggered in the morning,

Buggered in the evening,

Buggered at supper time,

If you get stuck in Menston,

You get buggered all the time.'

I visited two people that morning and two that afternoon. The first woman was deafblind; culturally deaf, she had later lost her sight. She was knitting and the needles were flying. She objected to my fumbling use of the deafblind manual alphabet and responded by pushing her needles at me. It wasn't a good start, but what else could she do? She was busy and an idiot was playing with her hands. After four years of monthly visits I eventually found how to develop a relationship with her but then, with no knowledge of mental illness and no language or diagnostic skills, I felt grossly inadequate. I then found, in the gardens, the big lumbering man I had seen while walking up the drive. Although amiable, our communication was negligible, just some nodding and smiling. I had quickly become adept at pretending to understand; that became a long-term skill.

Being a closed institution, lunch meant walking half a mile back to the main road to enjoy fish and chips in Harry Ramsden's famous restaurant. After I finished, I asked a man opposite if he minded if I smoked. 'Don't mind if you go up in bloody flames lad', he replied. I had more to learn than just deaf culture.

The others I visited were also mysteries. One woman was wary and angry. She seemed to be shouting at me, but I could not understand her. The fourth person seemed completely disinterested. He had, I later learned, been in High Royds for years and had become totally institutionalised. (Nine years later, three of the four had left, with one taking over from Mr Darville as the organisation's caretaker.)

On Saturday, after opening the offices at 9am I did various odd jobs until I could leave, three hours later. At noon, I set off for my first deaf cricket match in Yorkshire. I had to lug the gear to Soldiers' Field at Roundhay Park and, as well as organising tea and paying the umpires, I played in the team. Unsure of how I had been selected, I made fifty and got five wickets on a deplorable pitch. A week later, I became team captain; the missioner had spoken. My deaf predecessor had to stand back. Understandably, he never forgave me. By evening, I was back in Albion Street. I had to help with activities such as calling bingo and setting up a film projector. The deaf people were not allowed to use any equipment and each activity had to be supervised. I wasn't just walking round the premises, I learned, I was on patrol. Even Jimmy, my boss was there until 9pm, dealing with those who wanted his help.

Sunday started later – at 5pm – when the church, curtained off from the main hall, had to be prepared, hymns chosen, books set out. The service was a short version of Anglican Evening Prayer, conducted by the missioner. I went to see how the service was performed. The experience was absorbing. Already a born again Christian, I longed to make the beautiful movements and intone the liturgy, signing rhythmically with the speech. It resonated with my uncertain ambition and personal emotional needs. The building was closed at 9pm and I was allowed to go home, to be ready to start again at 9.30 the next morning.

∾

So what was I to make of my first seven days? That first week was completely overwhelming and I was in no position to ask questions about my experiences. Meeting the Darby and Joan club had been truly horrific. In the singular world I had entered new personalities were a focus of great interest and the unblinking gazes quickly became familiar and normal. Communication was entirely visual; look away for a millisecond and crucial information was missed. I had no language at that stage and no status either – my naval officer's accent meant nothing and I had no social tools to help create an impression. The experience was raw and formative. I was frightened and tempted to turn to avoidance. The old anxieties of school returned. I knew I had to find new survival techniques but had little idea how hard this would be.

I didn't know what to tell those who asked what I did for a living. I'd applied to be the trainee welfare officer. I worked beside the 'Lady Welfare'. I had seen the words 'missioner' and 'superintendent' used for Jimmy Hudson, my boss. I was confused, so were others. The titles, I learned, came from the origins of the work, dating back more than one hundred years.

The first organisations to care for (and control) deaf people appeared towards the end of the Napoleonic wars, in 1815. Young deaf people leaving schools set up a decade earlier had nothing

Clergy white 'tabs'

to do. They misbehaved, so charitable institutions were established to deal with the 'problem'. With religious roots, the purpose was regarded as a 'mission', so those in charge became 'missioners'. Deaf people created a sign for them – drawing the white 'tabs' of protestant clergymen's white collar. This remains a generic description of social or welfare workers. Potentially confusingly, it also represents 'church' and 'club for the deaf'.

Established in the 1850s as the Yorkshire Association for the Care of the Adult Deaf and Dumb, the organisation merged with the Leeds Institution for the Indigent and Industrious Blind in 1876. The first deaf missioner, Colin Campbell, arrived from Glasgow in 1856 but the organisation was, some thirty-five years later, still among the first for deaf people and active in helping found other groups in the region. The Leeds Incorporated Institution for the Blind and the Deaf and Dumb, as it became known, moved into newly-built premises at 135 Albion Street in 1878. Over the years, as local authorities had taken over services for blind people, the remit of the organisation had been reduced. When I arrived, this was limited to deaf people and an administrative office looking after charity for the blind.

Line drawing of the Institution from 1890

For many years, looking back to that first week, I wondered why learning to finger spell was my first assignment. Now, I think it clearly reflects the attitudes of the time – and how they had evolved. Finger spelling uses someone's first language alphabet literally spelt out on the hands. It is attributed to the Venerable Bede, who lived from about 673 until 735. A millennium later, in the eighteenth century, the French Abbé Charles-Michel de l'Épée is recorded as using a two-handed alphabet to teach deaf children. Two hundred years on I was learning, not the language of deaf people, but something quite alien to many members of the signing community. Clarifying English was a major part of the missioner's work. How could I build relationships if I was using alien communication? Some deaf people did have English, but they were the better educated and less likely to seek help.

Other common requirements of the time reinforced this. Everyone had to speak when communicating with deaf people. I found this inhibited and restricted my personal development as a communicator. This instruction made a nonsense of what should have been suitable and effective communication with deaf people – British Sign Language (BSL). Another assumption was that deaf people without English were poor communicators. Sign language was 'deaf and dumb talk'. On training courses, missioners, with hearing, depicted the language as a joke, like patronising yokels. This learning process led to a form of communication that could be called 'missioner speak' – and was most evident in church. Since the missions began, the religious signs had evolved to look very rhythmic and emotionally appropriate. I still don't know whether such language was fully understood or even if it was important. I wondered whether it reflected the historic use of Latin, both to separate priest and people and to control through exclusion (as seems so apparent with hindsight). Many years later, when the campaign to promote BSL was progressing, I was asked to explain what it was. My best answer was that BSL was the native language of deaf people in the UK. Unfortunately, my attempts to clarify this by demonstrating 'missioner talk' and then stopping to mouth words while aping BSL often failed as I met the dismissive 'you mean deaf and dumb talk' reaction.

My over-riding impression of that first week was that deaf people had to be managed; they did little for themselves but had high expectations of what should be done for them, an arrangement I accepted for six years. Every activity was intended to objectify deaf people. Both the organisation's hearing trustees and those who used its services knew well what was expected of them. The trustees gave and the users took, with the missioner as intermediary, defining attitudes and behaviours for both and maintaining the power relationships.

I had much to learn and could only do so on the job. The other staff seemed so competent and comfortable in their roles that I was left feeling frightened and inadequate. I had wanted the job and, even without qualifications or confidence, I was now on my way to becoming a missioner. Luckily for me, my academic deficiencies would be hidden by deaf people's poor education.

During the next few months I learnt how to survive – how to escape from the anxiety and stress of not being able to be myself, not having a language and not being able to use humour. I didn't know how non-verbal humour worked. All the social skills from my middle-class professional home and background were useless. I had to re-invent myself as a strict rationer of social benefits and a moulder of actions and behaviour. I would become part of the system that consigned deaf people to negative feelings and low aspirations.

I was confused. On one level, the only differences I could see were that others were deaf while I could hear. I didn't want division. I didn't have any template to work from, a ploy that I now believe made life easier for the organisation's management because I would quickly accept the status quo. I was told not to become familiar with deaf people, to think of myself as different. I didn't appreciate the reasoning. Ironically, and despite being so young, I had already experienced social division. Getting my commission in the navy had forced a sudden transformation. I could, however, see that the Royal Navy had both a history and a hierarchy which explained the very different ranks and their roles. I was in a setting without that background. Against more than one hundred years of institutional attitudes and management, I was a very different person in the lives of deaf people. I had to learn why. And that I had to start from scratch for myself.

I started by adopting a range of historical conventions. I wore suits and ties. My language, both in the choice of words and how I used them, had to be 'missioner-like'; I deliberately didn't learn to swear in sign language for a long time. (After many wasted years, Martin Colville's book *Signs of a Sexual Nature* let me into the very rich erotic world created by deaf people's imaginations.) I wasn't allowed to go out with deaf girls or to drink with anybody in city centre pubs, as this would have set a bad example for the community. This distinction became clearer when, decades later, I was asked by a woman of my own age if I had 'fancied' any of them (the girls). 'All of them,' I replied. What else could I say?

Everything I did had to conform to a model of behaviour appropriate for someone who had to be in charge, whatever happened. Deaf people had to know their place so they could be managed. Reinforcing that was part of the job. Nothing developmental was ever considered. Nobody said anything at all about helping deaf people become independent or to grow at all. The deaf community had its own well-defined ways of life too, with rules laid down over the previous one hundred and fifty years. Many deaf boarding schools generated acquiescent personalities and missions continued the institutionalisation.

In four years I learned enough to become a qualified welfare officer for the deaf. My post was not unique. Around the country, about thirty people worked in organisations set up to manage the deaf. I met them on a training course each year to be told who and what 'deaf people' were. We learned how they should be treated in terms of social lives, employment, protection from blame and their defence. It was universal: the deaf are like this, they must behave like that, they must marry one another and form a solid community that can be easily managed and described. Compliance and conformity, even oppression, were paramount.

With hindsight, deafness then seems synonymous with stupidity and intellectual stagnation. Some tasks were tacitly prohibited. Deaf people did very little for themselves in the clubs so I had to go to league football, table tennis and snooker meetings to take decisions for them. In church, they could not clean communion plates or prepare food; only a selected few could pour the tea. No one on any management committee was deaf, they could not be trusted to be confidential. They were not allowed their own committees to decide what they wanted to do or organise. Missioners ran the dances, the church, the holidays, the outings and the social occasions and very little happened without a welfare officer present. 'Kind carers' even had to be in sports team photographs.

Was this a huge social conspiracy or a burning missionary desire to provide 'something of a life for these unfortunate creatures'? Details of work during four years of trial and error later provided some kind of an answer.

Away from work I quickly made friends. They gave me not just a needed alternative to this 'other world' but a whole new way of living, thinking and being. I quickly moved out of the hostel when I found a one-bedroomed flat at 2 West Hill Terrace (opposite the YMCA), costing thirty shillings a week. The others living there were very friendly: an artist teacher, Shan (Sian) Edwards, who later became my son's godmother, Robin Russell, a psychologist from Armley prison and Neville Atkinson, a brilliant musician. We had cocoa evenings and made musique concrète reinforcé (reinforced concrete music – popular at the time). The people and the happenings were as healthily different from work as they could be.

A group of young Jewish professionals also accepted me, perhaps because with very black hair and using my hands while talking, I looked similar. I was particularly lucky to meet a chiropodist and radical thinker called Jack Marks over lunch in the Delmore café in Upper Briggate. Jack was an established active member of the Communist Party of Great Britain. He made no attempt to influence my politics but introduced me to his loving and extended family and friends, including my future brother-in-law Tony Davy and, through him, my future wife Jill. I suspect the family thought an arranged marriage to a speech therapist would be suitable, even though she was training in London. They were right. A legacy from my mother helped the courtship by paying for visits to London. My mother had been to Leeds to see me after talking to the Reverend Wally Brown, the missioner in Exeter. She felt the work suited me and provided wonderful support. Although they never met, two weeks before my mother died I told her over the phone about Jill.

Jack and his family represent the best of Leeds – diverse, cultured and open and very different from Exeter. From Jack I learned to appreciate Jewish humour, then a must for anyone wanting to really enjoy aspects of Leeds' culture.

Many of those I met then have remained loved and treasured friends whose perspectives helped me think about my career. Their company and advice helped me balance deaf happenings with the rest of my life. These were stimulating times and Leeds was culturally a great place that I never, emotionally, left.

3

Sandwich Courses

Throw it at the wall
What do I throw? Myself?
What makes the wall? The wall of deafness.
The physical and sensational
The social interaction
The psychological complexity
The perceived pathological
The institutional containment
The cultural rigidity
The thrower committed but self determined
The establishment apprehension
The Christian missionary
The Liberal missionary
The Medical missionary
Received, historical failure
Required change
Determined containment, managed response
Managed behaviour
Fear of exposure, guilt
Paradigms of normality
What a loaded dice to throw.

So many aspects and effects of deafness confronted me, initially as I trained and then as my career progressed, that the verse overleaf seems appropriate to express the emotions and challenges. Years later, I am still learning, finding insights, trying not to claim any arrogant full understanding of the implications of profound pre-lingual deafness.

My training in Leeds passed with an almost daily anxiety that I was never quite fulfilling the perceived role of a traditional carer. The covert assumption was that I would never fully enter a deaf world – as I came from a 'hearing' family. I was also middle class and the culture I was trying to understand was predominantly working class. I was an enthusiastic beginner trying to enter a different way of life. Deaf people hid my dyslexic condition and my poor English skills, especially my fear of writing. They had similar problems because of poor education, so most could not detect my inadequacy. I also had the advantages of spoken language and experience. Even so, I had lots to learn, but thinking about my work in distinct elements made the process easier.

INTERPRETING

Juxtaposing sandwich making for the elderly with counting on one's hands for community bingo seems bizarre beside becoming an interpreter, yet all three skills seemed to be vital parts of the process of becoming a qualified worker with deaf people. The first two are visibly helpful examples of care, but communicating and interpreting was very different. Here were challenges beyond my experience. They demand the greatest professionalism – such as the intense language skills I took years to refine. Eventually I had to grasp medical and legal terminology and procedures as well as the appropriate signs. Transforming jargon into signs involved fumbling and stumbling but it was essential. During those four years, I had no sign language tuition. It wasn't taught anywhere and no one knew how to teach it. It had to be absorbed, almost by osmosis. I learned most in church – as services were both said and signed. Minimal skills do not, however, enable genuine communication.

As professional interpreters hadn't really been invented, such responsibilities were part of the welfare remit. Fortunately, I found each different setting fascinating and exciting as deaf people took me everywhere from hospitals, doctors' surgeries, dental schools, employment exchanges, estate agents and building societies to more mundane shops and offices. However, I never went to court during my training years, except to pay in fines for clients. The skills required for that work were too complex for a trainee.

As 'welfare', I rapidly realised I was also expected to assume total responsibility for dealing with other organisations, so I had to know deaf people's problems better than they did themselves as they were generally excluded from what went on. Normal, individual lives could easily be changed dramatically, especially in medical settings. Doctors and nurses expected me to explain someone's state of heath. They'd ask 'what's the problem?' highlighting the difference between welfare officers and interpreters. In the twenty-first century, interpreters ideally need a first degree in sign communication boosted by training specific to each profession, but in the 1950s and 60s, everyone coped, for better or for worse – and litigation was unknown. Once, a consultant said 'Martin, tell her to take her clothes off'. I did. Rightly, the woman decided against the continued presence of 'welfare'; our involvement could be limited, but not often.

Another time, a consultant indicated that he would perform a placebo operation on a deaf person's leg. The deaf person was constantly complaining about the pain but the doctor could find nothing wrong. Being privy to such information was new to me. So was dealing with medical euphemism and sensitivity when I had to try to explain a 'poor prognosis' to someone terminally ill.

The onus of such complexity and responsibility can only be assessed in retrospect and every experience affected my perspective. I became increasingly aware how little the medical profession understood, so I later championed such awareness as essential for medical students and, nowadays, a client's symptoms are none of an intepreter's business.

In 1950, there were about two hundred and fifty missioners combining interpreting with welfare work. Being an 'expanded communicator' was part of the work that felt very real and sustained my professional satisfaction. Communicating with the hearing world is vital for deaf people. Today, interpreting is a 'freeing-up' profession that eases this process, through dedicated units and, by 2014, there were more than a thousand qualified practitioners in the UK. I believe the interpreter role was one of the ways missioners could perpetuate their control. If deaf people couldn't speak for themselves, a sense of power could be exercised. A decreasing number of survivors of such paternalism still expect interpreters to be 'friends', and struggle with the new breed of independent interpreters, finding them distant, indifferent or even aloof, simply because they are trying to be professional.

However, whatever the language, interpreters have the responsibilities of avoiding the temptation to manipulate that accompanies such great power. They convey the good and bad. I have been hugged for telling a woman she was pregnant and beaten and bloodied for telling a man he was sacked. The diversity of the situations and subjects where communication was needed were real professional bonuses for me. My general knowledge rapidly expanded and I felt appreciated in so many different places. I had a real job, with respect and social influence. Great satisfaction came from learning how to get round bigger institutions as a 'known professional'. After a year or two, I got to know people well enough to avoid queues and long waits. Earning the respect of gatekeepers in secure settings such as mental hospitals and prisons won me easier access there too.

Personal relationships were also crucial. Hours spent waiting in hospitals and social security offices meant you got to know your 'deaf flock', as they were often patronisingly called. Critical settings with intimate information shared and held on trust produce life-long and strong relationships, good and bad, and often very powerful. Once, for instance, the teenage daughter of a deaf person was seriously ill in hospital and could only mumble. She had tubes everywhere. Her mother wanted to speak to her and I had to lean over the bed to try to distinguish what she said and then sign the messages to her distraught mother. How privileged is that? Even now, after forty years, I draw warmth and affection from that episode, which ended happily with the girl's recovery. Sometimes leaving oneself out of the situation was impossible, especially when you had to show care as 'welfare'.

Being needed was a huge confidence and emotional boost for me and essential at work. Words I understood and concepts I could grasp. Writing was unnecessary so my poor spelling and academic limitations were not exposed. My sign language skills grew, but without fluency; I really needed someone to sit down and tell me what the language was about. Using my hands to communicate felt incongruous and, at first, frightening. Sometimes I watched my boss being less formal, signing without speech, in a way that made all around him relax and laugh. He was entertaining his flock in his, and their, first language – BSL. I did not understand the language he was using and it wasn't explained. Indeed, then, the term BSL had not entered the general vocabulary, nor even the deaf vocabulary, and I was still floundering in a world for which there was no adequate description. It was fascinating, however, to watch and try to copy my boss and his incredible finger spelling skills when he was in formal mode. His fingers flew with great accuracy – not with BSL, but with English performed on the hands. Each is very different.

(BSL has evolved into formal and informal styles. The formal requires a straight-backed head-up look, a kind of authoritarian pose. The informal needs lower shoulders and flexible wrists with much more facial expression. At the beginning, I had learn to spell quickly and blend in a few appropriate signs, a form known as 'sign-supported English', which I later called 'missioner talk'. It followed established English word sequences, rather than BSL grammar, and was the language missioners used and expected to be understood.)

I had, I discovered, a physical problem with signing. My childhood fall from a tree, resulting in a broken wrist where the bones locked, caused lifelong problems in my choice of employment. Sign language requires free movement of the upper body. My signing became strained as my frozen wrist induced muscular tension, hunching the shoulder. This, accompanied by an anxious expression, appeared incongruous, obstructing communication and drawing comments from deaf people.

Interpreting and the use of sign language in all its aspects affected everything else I did and the perspective that emerged. Learning more is still joyful, boosted by access to this product of rich, non-verbal imagination that wouldn't have been possible in any other walk of life. Indeed, I can now express humour – but the reactions can be unpredictable. When a young woman said: 'You are funny man', I like to think she meant my humour. Those of us who can hear and grow up learning to think in words take this for granted. Those who do not hear do not have this language foundation; they have an alternative, non-verbal communication. This imagination is as rich as any so, perhaps unsurprisingly, universal gestures became the core of sign language. (Today, electronic communication repeatedly reminds us that the tone of voice – and adverbs – are essential if we want to avoid mis-understanding or upsetting one another.)

BEGGING AND AWARENESS RAISING

Before starting this work, I had never even thought about having to beg on behalf of the deaf, but it quickly became obvious that it was vital. Nowadays, this is deemed to be fundraising, publicity or even awareness training. Even though local authority funding for social welfare was increasing, more money was still required for 'treats'. Requests had to be nuanced. Writing to Bertram Mills' Circus, I described the senior citizens club members as 'those people for whom only the visual spectacle can lift the sense of social isolation' – and got thirty free front row seats for a matinee. On the day, at 4pm and with half an hour of the performance to go, they got up and walked out. It was their tea time – and that never changed. Having pleaded their need, I was left with an empty row of expensive seats and much embarrassment. But food came first; it usually does in deaf society.

I learned how to manipulate others. The general ethos was to elicit sympathy towards an emphasised image of inadequacy. Deaf people had to be regarded as needy objects, worthy of the financial support required by servicing organisations such as the missions. Local authorities and the public were the sources of funds. I wrote to Leeds shops with blanket requests for raffle prizes or goods for jumble sales and then had to go and collect everything. I found this quite humiliating. I disliked asking and it was not what I had expected, but it taught me about this aspect of the history of deaf people and the organisations serving them. Traditionally, they had relied on charity and the kindness of donors, contributing to perceptions of deaf people as receivers not givers; the deserving poor, hapless and helpless. In the late 1950s that still seemed unlikely to change.

Jumble sales raised useful money for holidays and Christmas presents so I had to learn to run them. I had to watch for professional thieves and make sure anything of real value was removed, to be used later as raffle prizes. The mobs were held back until the doors opened, then the rush was on. I had to look under the trestle tables as children crawled underneath and nicked stuff from below. When it was over, deaf people were freely allowed to pick what they wanted. I did to. I got some golf shoes with white flashes that I covered with polish. When I took out the studs I realised that the shoes let in water, but times were hard. I also found what my friends called a 'flashers' mac' in one pile of left-over clothes.

I regularly had to give talks, again hoping for donations, but – importantly – public speaking boosted my confidence and self-esteem. My first talk was to a group of elderly women in Stanningley. I asked my boss what I should talk about and received the advice that if I ran run out of material I should teach them to finger spell. Much had to be made of the maltreatment of deaf people. Historically, babies diagnosed as deaf were, allegedly, variously thrown into the Tiber, exposed to die on the mountainsides in Greece or, nearer home, drowned in the River

Derwent. Such tales, even if witches were mentioned, evoked little sympathy however truthful they may have been. Incidentally, I never saw anyone at a talk I knew to be deaf.

In Stanningley, needless to say, I had to resort to the finger spelling demonstration. I showed them what to do but was, of course, the wrong way round for them to copy me so, I turned my back on the sixty women and told them to copy my hand movements. I demonstrated by raising my hands above my head and started to spell ABC. Hearing much heavy breathing and stretching, I turned to see the women trying to get their hands above their heads. I can't remember if we got a donation.

Once, I received a request for a talk about 'Deaf and Dumbs, P.S. we like a good laugh'. The letter came from Headingley Baptists' old people's group. When I told a Methodist group in Chapel Allerton about the isolation of deaf people and their loneliness, a man jumped up and told me I was wrong. He had worked with a deaf person for years who had been treated very well by his workmates. I asked him for the deaf person's name as I felt I probably knew him. 'Oh,' said the man, 'I don't know his name, we just called him Dummy.'

That didn't feel too incongruous then and I felt duty bound to conform, even though this contributed to deaf people being seen as objects of pity, rather than as people, but it was what the good missioner did to bring succour to his flock. One missioner, now famous in the annals of deaf culture, used a hurdy-gurdy and a monkey to raise money for his organisation – the sign language descriptions of this are hilarious. I also felt most people were, and are, indifferent to such talks. Whatever one said had no lasting influence. Like many, I became defensive as I failed to change people's attitudes, even though I didn't realise that for many years. I believe many committed to working with disabled, or marginalised, people mistakenly think they are the only ones who really understand.

Begging taught me how to play on public sympathy, just as the management committees and national bodies did. The dichotomy was clear: how do you promote a supportive organisation without condemning the individual to being an object of charity? I believe that the state, through taxation, should provide the money necessary to pay for equality of access and opportunity.

JOB FINDING

Getting deaf people jobs was a high priority, not least because part of the organisation's historical raison d'être was a commitment to providing work for the blind and encouraging indigent deaf people to work. From mid-nineteenth century origins, missions spent much time finding jobs for their charges. I followed this well-defined path. A good missioner was a good job finder. Finding jobs or 'placement' as it was termed, fulfilled often obscure and apparently competing needs.

The system was well organised. Before leaving school at sixteen, each young person would have had some contact with the organisation or 'deaf club' and their details were known and recorded, benefitting both parties. The leavers got information about all the social activities and church worship as well as post-school education such as basic English and maths (historically taught by the missioner and paid for by the local education authority). Some boys clearly had potential in the football and cricket teams before they left school. Fourteen-year-old Leslie Townend, for example, played regularly for the Leeds deaf cricket team and later, as an adult, captained the England deaf team on a tour to Australia.

During each summer term, meetings were arranged between deaf school headmasters, their deputies, each leaver's parents and the missioner. One particular headmaster, who had a reputation in the deaf community for hitting children with a small cricket bat if they used sign language, seemed happy to be passing on his charges. The meetings would usually start with the deputy talking about a young person's achievements. Then I would ask the school leaver in sign language what they wanted to do. The prevailing deaf education philosophy then meant only promoting speech and lip reading so neither the headmaster nor the deputy had signed communication with the children. The parents couldn't communicate with their children effectively either as they too had been counselled not to use manual language. Everyone seemed pleased to see someone (me) who could, and under the circumstances, was allowed, to communicate with the young person through signing. Consequently, we were the only two people in the meeting really communicating.

Despite this formality, the children had learned and kept up signing as vital in the playground, even though it was never allowed in the classroom. Later, visiting a school in Oldham I saw two boys signing at the back of the class. One said: 'good place deaf club, can sign there.'

I took part in lots of these sessions once I learned enough. I was always quietly thrilled by the pupils' responses as they were invariably positive. The work was powerful as, at last, the young had someone who could talk to them. Here again, language was crucial. For the first time in someone's life, the two systems, oral and non-oral, the signers and the non-signers, clashed. By then however, the young person's needs were paramount. A quick chat to a leaver established a friendship while the parents were relieved to find someone who could help them then and in the future. I would take the school leavers' details and register them on a social services list. The council funding meant the missioner was effectively running a social services department. Consequently, annual returns had to be submitted, detailing how many deaf and hard of hearing people were receiving services. More people meant more money, so the process worked well. The school leaving process let schools merrily pass on their failures while the missioners delightedly got recruits for the deaf club and their official reports.

I met many people who did not think of themselves as deaf until they left school. Some were frightened that this was the end of life. Their parents could not talk to them in their preferred language and they had never had meaningful chats with any other adults, leaving the missioner in a prime situation to begin their social education, as well as any further education. This unique role opened the door to a managed life, a set of taught realities, which spelt out 'I am deaf and this is what I do and don't do'.

Everyone expected work to be available. The boys went into joinery, bakery, French polishing, shoe repairing and, in Leeds, the clothing industry. The girls, if they were bright, went into copy typing, tracing, sewing and other jobs which did not require good English. (Deaf school leavers' reading ages were, on average, those of eight-year-olds.) The then diverse manufacturing industry in Leeds provided much semi-skilled work so no one had to wait long before finding work with a well-established company such as Montague Burton. They employed more than thirty deaf people at their huge Hudson Road factory while the Public Benefit Company, on Vicar Lane, employed twenty-five deaf people as boot and shoe repairers. Schools offered jobs for their past pupils. Non-speaking failures worked in the Leeds deaf school kitchen, while partially deaf school leavers were sometimes taken on as non-teaching assistants.

Part of the placement officer's job was to take each leaver along for interview, sell his or her potential skills and settle them in. Choosing which leaver and firm to put together required thought. You never took anyone to a regular employer whom you thought might be difficult or would spoil the deaf reputation. The range of placements really depended upon the success or failure of the education system and the traditional and limited range of employment reflected the very poor results of a system in place since the turn of the century.

Placement took up much time and needed good sales skills. Deaf people came to the office if they lost their jobs while the employers rang if there were problems and the Department of Employment was delighted when jobs were found. The missioner could cut another notch on his belt and report a successful placement to the committee; all neat and tidy as another deaf person had become a client, and a dependent one. Placements served the organisation's needs.

My cynicism here is deliberate. Thinking about the school leaver meetings in retrospect is alarming. The attitudes reveal much about the socialisation of deaf people at the time, including having untrained officers, like me, making random decisions about their abilities and their futures. However, placement continued as a mainstream part of the work until social work training changed, many years later.

WELFARE

The welfare role was regarded as 'do everything you are asked to do', based on the expectation that, as 'welfare', I knew everything and could solve every problem. All a deaf person had to do was to throw the problem at my door and walk away. The list was endless and really diverse, from domestic violence, child abuse, window repairs, long toe nail problems, mental illness, disputes with neighbours to the removal of evil spirits; almost everything a deaf person could not handle, because they didn't have the experience or spoken language skills. Some demanded specialist skills, while others called for wit, imagination and lateral thinking.

Much abuse in the home or boarding schools was never investigated and revealed as it would be today. Protecting the secrets of the deaf and their families was important, as was presenting those with financial needs to management committees as worthy of grants and other benefits. Being able to solve, or seem to solve, their problems was viewed as 'good welfare'. The missioner's response cut out options and deliberately no questions were asked. Even marriages were held together by the word of the missioner. The job seemed much akin to the realm of colonial officers of the empire whose word was law. Such regime controllers defined their own truths. When once I asked an intelligent deaf woman what she considered to be the truth, she replied: 'What the missioner says'. The approach allowed deaf people to negate all responsibility for their own affairs. I remember one man asking me to go with him to the building society. 'Which one?' I asked, 'and where?' His response was dismissive: 'Old missioner know; you no good.' Similarly, when I was helping one deaf man deal with the police, previous offences were mentioned. 'You tell them I can't remember,' I was told.

I had many tasks and systems to learn. One was how to deal with deaf tramps, many of whom roamed the country then. Consequently, each organisation had a 'tramp book'. The tramp would appear at the welfare office where names were recorded.

He (never she) would be given two shillings and sixpence and then be asked where they were going next. Usually they got a bus fare as well. Tramps were often difficult, freethinking spirits not easy to manage so this got them out of the area. Sometimes, if the missioner in the next parish was a friend, a call would be made to let them know who was on their way.

I do not know of another professional occupation where most of the clients know one another and meet regularly, so such intimacy affected the professional response. If we didn't comply with a request quickly, everyone in the pubs and deaf clubs would know that 'welfare' would not help. This potential for ransom had to be tackled; not complying caused major conflict and endless argument.

Church

Donning a cassock and standing in front of a gazing congregation was also in the job description. Becoming part of the worship brought a new and galvanising perspective to my life; on the surface an honourable task, pure, real and self-gratifying. Each week, in training, I watched with awe and respect how bringing a spiritual dimension into deaf people's lives was achieved. The artistry was amazing and the stagecraft highly professional, reminding me of my earlier theatrical interests. As a young Christian it strengthened my need for fulfilment as a missioner.

I learned sign language by watching and listening – and church was the best place. Not a natural, I tried hard. Despite the historical explanations, I found the language hard to absorb. Without a proper understanding of the derivation or syntax of signs or the underlying philosophy, I found it too complex. I had to learn to mould the two languages, English and sign language, together. Everything was spoken or sung and interpreted. I rehearsed in front of a mirror with the order of service and slowly I was allowed to participate.

After about a year, I was dispatched to Keighley to take a harvest festival service. I practised and practised. Sign and word perfect I arrived at the mission where I had been told the service would take place. 'Not here,' they said. 'Over at Methodists'. I went to the chapel and found out I was not to take the service, only interpret it. I was to follow the minister. My learnt service was worthless. I fumbled my way through his prayers but when it came to the hymns he announced his, and I signed mine. The hearing sang theirs and I tried to finish my signing on the same beat. I like to think the minister never knew.

Signing for Canon Howard Hamilton

Over time, physically, emotionally and spiritually, performing the services became deeply satisfying. After forty minutes the outpouring produced a feeling best described as orgasmic. No wonder I went back. I was learning a powerful role in which the language, style and performance of the missioner and the physical presence required were like that of an actor. The missioner played the lead while the deaf people were the passive audience. I got the picture. Questioning this, or the terminology, was, and is, a source of personal conflict. Even now, fifty years on, I miss the adrenalin rush and fulfilment.

Perhaps it was this longing that persuaded me, at the end of my initial training in Leeds, that my skills needed testing – and missionary work with deaf people in India appealed. I had become comfortable with the Church of England and, considering myself a committed Christian, I applied to the Church Missionary Society (CMS). Being my fiancée, Jill was interviewed as well – but separately. I faced rigorous interrogation to verify my commitment. Jill said she found the experience quite alarming. The determining factor was one's strength of faith; money didn't come into it, as missionaries were expected to raise the money to finance their calling. My interviewer was encouraging; the CMS would consider us if I went to college for a year, followed by twelve months in India. Jill would follow me to college and then join me a year later, after which we would have to wait a further year before seeking permission to marry. The sexual freedom of the sixties had not permeated our conventional middle-class life and we felt that three years was too long to wait; the appeal of missionary work was outweighed by other desires.

SPORT AND SOCIAL LIFE
The job advertisement had mentioned religion and sport, but I had no idea I would become responsible for all the deaf club's sporting activities. I'd heard of 'muscular Christianity' without realising that deaf people would command my evenings and weekends, but this quickly became the dominant aspect of my work. Sport was a huge part of the organisation's life: everyone

who attended had to be active and the responsibility lay with the trainee welfare officer – me. The healthy agenda for the job stretched to helping with youth clubs, walking clubs and organising dances.

Deaf cricket team circa 1980, I am front row, centre

I was expected to pretend I was an all-round sportsman, with universal knowledge and proficiency. I had never played snooker before or any other indoor sports, such as darts and dominoes. I had to learn indoor bowls and table tennis too. When, in September 1957, the cricket season ended, football – the most important game – took over. The Leeds Deaf Football Club had a proud reputation both locally and nationally. The club had, for fifty years, supplied players for the national and the deaf Olympic teams, including brothers Walter and Alan Chapman, George Jackson, Derek Walker and Leslie Townend. Even though I had never played (association) football, I was told to take over the training of the team. During the first warm-up, in a local gym, national team player Derek Walker rapidly realised I had little to offer, using a sign well-understood by both deaf and hearing people. But, I had to persist; it was part of my job. A run around Woodhouse Moor I could manage and I was given a place in the team. My appearance as a full back against Meanwood Trinity in the Allied Churches League went into the club's history. A few minutes after kick-off, Trinity forced a corner. I knew I had to defend and waited in the penalty area. The ball floated over and I ran towards it, jumping upwards in classic rugby union style. I caught the ball, landed, dug my heel into the turf and shouted 'mark', still holding the ball. The whistle sounded and the referee pointed to the penalty spot. I will never forget my teammates' expressions. For years, one of them, Leslie Pickergill, who later became the organisation's caretaker, never let a conversation go by without telling the story: 'Never seen before,' he'd say, forever having me at an embarrassed disadvantage.

As a rugby player, I always disliked football, but my reputation did give me some status. Later in life, one deaf opponent re-enacted my young bravado, dramatically mimicking me knocking others out of my way with elbows and shoulders. Nothing went unseen by those entirely reliant on their vision.

Playing in the team sat most incongruously with my role as an authority figure, helping referees impose discipline. In this 'hearing' league, refs had to wave a white hankie when they blew the whistle. I had to sprint over and interpret cautions or explanations as if the deaf players could not understand them, causing much conflict and setting me apart from my teammates. This conflict came to a head while getting changed after one match. Without warning, one team member, Jimmy Nasser, lent over and tweaked my right nipple. I grimaced and everyone else laughed. I had been known as 'Fisticuffs Smith' on the rugby field and, anywhere else, I would have responded differently. However, I felt constrained by my role, which certainly did not involve fighting with clients. I smiled and dressed quickly. No protocols covered such incidents, so I decided to keep my distance.

The winter months were full of the indoor activities in which I was expected to be centrally involved. I played in a table tennis league and joined snooker and billiard league management committees on behalf of the club, going to meetings and reporting back to the players. I even learned to brush and press the baize, heating huge irons on the kitchen hob, testing them for temperature and then using them speedily to achieve the best surface. Such involvement displayed care and concern for the community's happiness and well-being while being, on reflection, totally unnecessary. A greater indoor games enthusiast, Harry Ledger, welcomed the opportunity to take over when I could delegate some tasks, doing everything with pleasure and with much better results.

During the following summers, as my missioner boss Jimmy Hudson was secretary of the British Deaf Sports Association, I was pulled into national sport. I had to train local athletes and assist with regional events. With no proper professional support and a rudimentary knowledge of sprinting, javelin and discus, I was some use but still felt inadequate. I asked if I could transfer from in-house welfare training to a full-time college sports course and become a better national trainer. Jimmy Hudson quashed the idea; I think I had probably become too useful to spend any time away. I continued trying to do my best but still felt deaf people were being let down.

I was, however, qualified to run the swimming club, which I did confidently. I had swum competitively at school and I also had lifesaving awards – which came in useful. I saved a lad called Warburton, a visiting choirboy from Leeds Parish Church, from drowning. His grateful parents gave me the huge sum, for those days, of ten pounds. I bought myself a watch, but ran into immediate disapproval; I was only doing my job and the money should have gone to the organisation.

I was also responsible for discipline on the premises and maintaining the expected standards. For example, anyone fighting was 'banished' – a well-established and effective means of control. What is more painful than being cut off from the only community with which you can communicate? Quite arbitrarily, letters would be delivered by hand, excluding someone from community activities. The 'clever deaf' were brought within the hierarchy with morsels of status or power. The control was enhanced because, even after an assault or criminal damage, the police were never involved; the missioner-superintendent had total authority. Over time, I learned from contemporaries and colleagues that this was widespread.

The job reminded me very much of a public school housemaster, so 'missioner' and 'superintendent' were apt job titles. Similarly, my responsibilities seemed endless. The six key elements seemed to fit uneasily together but this had evolved generations earlier, when many institutions were established to control anyone who appeared different. Mental hospitals held a whole range of people who flouted, or appeared to flout, the serious social conventions of the time; being an unmarried mother or having epilepsy were sufficient offences, not just amongst the deaf but also the wider population. Deaf people who transgressed or were socially disruptive could end up in such settings. That many were incarcerated for no good reason became a later professional interest.

4

A Change of Scenery

FOUR YEARS OF LEARNING, RATHER than formal training had brought some success. Despite my historic lack of academic prowess, I scraped through the final exams of the Deaf Welfare Examination Board in the early 1960s. Established in 1927, the syllabus included subjects thought relevant to the life and history of deaf people. The exams included a sign language practical with written papers covering 'who' and 'what' deaf people were, their language, expectations and social history as well as an emphasis on how their religious needs should be met. The papers confirmed traditional attitudes, referring to deaf people as 'Your Flock'.

Those who took the secular exams got certificates while those who added the religious curriculum were awarded diplomas. Eventually, both qualifications were recognised by local authorities. They imparted eligibility for membership of the National Council of Missioners and Welfare Officers for the Deaf. The Royal National Institute for the Deaf (RNID, now known as Action on Hearing Loss) kept records of everyone who qualified, and their marks, in their library. Mine reflected my continuing difficulties with exams and written work.

Officially qualified, my salary included annual increments sanctioned by the RNID. These professional positions all seemed very different. Each organisation that provided 'training' had its own particular emphasis, determined largely by its location and the missioner's personal interests. Pastoral care was greater in regional towns, while in cities, where deaf people used the facilities more often, work and community life were paramount.

Less formally, I learned about managing deaf culture. I accepted, without question, the status quo between carers and the cared presented to me. I could enforce discipline, 'sell' the disability, raise funds, speak in public and arrange placements. I could play snooker and billiards, blind whist and run bingo sessions. I could show the films I thought suitable for Saturday nights. In formal missioner style, I conducted church services, baptisms, weddings and funerals. I could fill in social security and benefit application forms. My developing intellectual ability and confidence grew from such experience. I had even started to understand working class survival.

However, dealing with mental health problems and emotional deprivation remained beyond me. My language was too shallow to distinguish between the normal and abnormal, nor did I have any experience of the courts and their particular requirements – interpreting and being an expert witness. I knew nothing of the media, the police, probation or education authorities.

Nevertheless, in 1961, with the qualification and enough skill and experience, I applied for, and got, a job as the deputy super-intendent of the Chester and North Wales Society for the Deaf. Based in Chester, the society had the statutory responsibility for the social welfare of deaf people across its catchment area.

Leaving Leeds was easy professionally. The intensity was becoming claustrophobic. Good counselling by Trevor Bone, the precentor of Leeds Parish Church, supported me through times of doubt and frustration over the seemingly disproportionate attention that deaf people demanded and got. He told me to absorb all the rich lessons around me. He was right. Socially, however, the move was more difficult. My leaving party occupied all three floors of the house where I lived. Friends came and went, eating, drinking and dancing for about three days and nights. I think my far back Devon lilt, cultural interests and dancing skills let me hold my own among those young, more wealthy professionals; I was only earning £600 a year (about £12,500 in today's terms).

I may have missed Leeds friends, but I still had Jill. After qualifying and a year working in Yorkshire, she got a job in Wrexham. Asked at her interview if she spoke Welsh, she said no. Embarrassingly, the panel chair suggested she should find a nice Welsh lad to teach her. We were married by Trevor Bone during my second year in Chester.

Our wedding day in 1962 – signing to deaf friends who turned up at the church

My move west across the Pennines coincided with the wider social changes of the 1960s when protests erupted against despised conventions, attitudes and behaviour. Free thinkers and freedom fighters triumphed with their 'modern' concepts of liberty. Professionally, work was to prove very different, evolving in a way that was both unbelievable and fascinating. In Chester, my salary doubled and the intensity disappeared. No one there provided such intense care as we had done in Leeds. Deaf people were less demanding and the club life was absent. I went from working an average sixty hours a week to thirty-seven.

Different pressures materialised however. On my first morning at the Northgate Street headquarters, I was refused access to client records. The secretary said the boss had told her not to give me the filing cabinet keys. Instead, I was handed a new hard-backed red file listing every deaf person in the area. I was to visit each of them, solve their problems and provide spiritual care – all part of the remit – but without any information about anyone's history.

The Chester HQ

Most surprisingly and strangest to me, the missioner could hardly sign. After my Leeds experience, I found this amazing, especially in a boss. I was accustomed to colleagues considered among the nation's best communicators. Any respect I had for the Chester organisation and its leading figures quickly vanished. I felt I wasn't wanted. I didn't know why, but I found this situation strangely exciting. My suspicions were confirmed after a few months, during a visit to Welsh-speaking Caernarfon. After repeated attempts to visit a man called Jones, whose house looked deserted, I went to the local police station. A helpful officer told me Mr Jones had died nine months earlier. I went to the county council offices and asked for copies of the reports submitted by the organisation. They indicated that Mr Jones was 'still' being anti-social, even after death. The missioner, a free church minister had, I thought, his own special communication channel with the Almighty.

Being unprepared was unhelpful. One damp and foggy day in Snowdonia, I thought I had found, at last, the person I was looking for. I had been told he was deafblind. Along the path to his home, I saw someone moving quickly though the fog. I got out of the way. A few moments later, the figure returned, carrying a bottle of milk. I followed and tried to communicate using signs and speech. I got no response. So I grabbed the man's hand and used the deafblind manual alphabet. I thought I was winning. He spelt back 'Do you speak Welsh?' 'No, sorry,' I said. 'Well bugger off and learn,' he told me abruptly. My doubts about not being wanted were further confirmed when I was sent to a council house on the edge of Chester. I waved a newspaper at the windows to attract attention, then the customary way of getting into a deaf person's house. When the door opened, I said I was from 'welfare'. He raised his fists and came towards me. I retreated rapidly. Back at the office, I asked my colleagues about him. They said this always happened. No one had thought to warn me.

The senior managers had a routine that started at about 9am. Archie, the welfare assistant, would take the society's Ford Consul to collect the boss (the missioner) and the chairman. After stopping for coffee at a good hotel, they would visit a deaf person's house, with prayers or the laying on of hands to cast out the evil spirits, which were deaf of course. After an adequate lunch and a snooze, they would make a second visit, before saying 'Home, Archie'. The two visits cost two salaries, expenses for three and fuel. I was taken along for such a day out, probably so I could be shown how good life could be if I behaved myself. The contrast to the dedication shown in Leeds was extreme.

Even the religious work was nominal, carried out in an office with a desk as an altar, or in a hired room in Bangor without any religious atmosphere. Services were held, but never Anglican communion. One Sunday a month, a welfare officer would drive sixty miles from Chester to Bangor to lead a service, as part of the mission to the Welsh deaf. Often no one was there, but the local authority could be told the work was being properly carried out. Each harvest festival, the good people of Chester gave fruit and gifts for the poor deaf and dumb. The staff chose the best for themselves and then delivered the rest during home visits. I felt I was working for a corrupt organisation where deaf people didn't matter; something had to be done.

After about a year, I began a crusade among the Cheshire establishment. With my contacts from home and the navy, I visited, among others, the county medical officer and the Lord Lieutenant, telling them of the corruption, as I saw it. As nothing was criminal, the response was negligible. When the management committee found out, I was hauled in front of them and told to behave so that I could have 'a job for life'. My punishment was to visit all the deaf people in Flintshire, without a car. That took six weeks of walking, sometimes twenty miles a day. I put messages through the office door but did not otherwise communicate. I was telephoned at home and asked to go in. I refused and only turned up on Sunday nights to take the evening service. I enjoyed myself, buoyed by self-righteous indignation. Soon however, I resolved that the protest was useless as no one cared enough to change anything, especially as the organisation had contracts with seven local authorities in Chester and north Wales. They seemed happy as long as they got professional reports.

As well as that salutary lesson, I learned about deaf people and their weakness in the face of unscrupulous 'hearing' people with greater English. One dedicated volunteer, Mr Evans, was a powerful example of what could be typical. He was intelligent and kind and travelled widely around north Wales on foot, train and bus during the late 1940s. He discovered many people living in isolation, usually after education at one of the deaf schools, either in Liverpool or Llandrindod Wells. He provided some care and support, and helped found the area's first deaf society. The National Assistance Act of 1948 allowed voluntary organisations to become local authority agencies, paid for their services. Deaf societies became better-established and more hearing people saw opportunities to be paid for deaf work. Councils wanted evidence of what was being financed, so reports became all-important. As Mr Evans could not write well and his English wasn't good enough, he was replaced.

What the work lacked in intensity, it made up for with driving – more than forty thousand miles a year. This gave me time to think about mental health and placements. Remembering my experiences at High Royds near Leeds, I asked the medical superintendent of the area's largest institution, Denbigh Hospital for Nervous Diseases, for permission to carry out some research. I wrote initially to ward staff asking if they would bring anyone they thought profoundly deaf to meet me. Sitting at a table I signed to try to get reactions. Despite this poor approach I elicited enough, over two days, to make a list of those I wanted to talk to at length. Eventually, I formed a group of those categorised as deaf. One man had been locked up for forty-two years. Using the sign language he had sustained, he told how, after leaving school, he was given a job on a building site. He knew nothing about work so, when he was told to carry heavy bricks, he threw one at the foreman. I had some successes in other areas – organising hospital clubs and support groups and starting to find work for deaf people to improve their status. When Vauxhall Motors opened a factory at nearby Ellesmere Port, I found a job there for an intelligent man called Doug Pane, probably the first of many to start breaking down the barriers to deaf people working with heavy machinery.

But the society provided me with no real challenges or looked to develop as an organisation. The time driving around almost half of Wales, influenced by the challenges to oppression blossoming in the sixties, inspired thoughts about how deaf people might become more self-determining. The Cheshire organisation had no deaf people on its management committee or running their own clubs. No national organisations had deaf executives; one hundred years of special education appeared to have produced little advancement. The challenge came to dominate my career.

While Chester represented professional stagnation, life was ideal for Jill and me, as a newly-married couple and we began our domestic life in reasonable comfort. We had time to establish friendships that have survived. We got to know Robin and Carey Samuel and estate agent John Palmer, who found us a flat to rent in Riversleigh, a big house in nearby Rossett. I joined Round Table and began to learn more about attitudes towards 'soft' welfare work. I gave lectures and talks to try to awaken interest in the needs of deaf people. This did not work directly, but my reputation for being well-intentioned was enhanced. My self-esteem and confidence improved further and my dyslexia anxiety diminished. I think Jill used her professional speech therapy skills to diagnose this very early in our marriage, probably during pillow talk. Life was comfortable and stress free, but unfulfilled. I needed to feel justified or useful. Moving on became important. When, in 1962, after three years in Chester, the post of super-intendent of the Oldham Society was advertised, I was raring to put some more radical ideas into practice.

Oldham's Society for the Deaf was based centrally, in the old Liberal club, near Alexandra Park. The community was warm and intense while the town itself was diverse with many different nationalities. After Chester, it felt real. As the superintendent, I was interviewed by the local media, felt important and was in charge, even though I didn't have any staff. The mission and the missioner-superintendent's accommodation were one and the same. The club and office were on the ground floor while the flat and church were up three flights of stairs. I could walk across the landing to start services, having donned my cassock, surplice and diploma hood. I took over from a clergyman whose parents had been deaf, whose well-trodden route to the priesthood had begun as a lay missioner. The organisation was stagnant so I easily appeared youthful and ambitious.

The Oldham Society building

The Oldham post also revealed that the missioner role was for not one but two – assuming that the wife would be involved as well. Jill had no official association with the organisation – working as an NHS speech therapist – so, much to our surprise, I had a request for her to accompany a woman to a breast cancer clinic. 'Why?' I asked. The missioner's wife always went with deaf women, I was told. Jill's interpreting skills were limited but she was still expected to support sensitive and delicate interactions between doctor and patient. This was what the missioner's wife did. Living in the community, refusing was difficult, especially as it would have been regarded as rejection.

Such experiences highlight the close and dependent relation-ships between worker and client group. How can you say no? You will probably see someone three times in a week, at church, perhaps a sewing group and at club night. What will refusing do to your reputation? How do you change attitudes and systems while still meeting needs? The culture embedded this expectation – that my wife and I were 'family', available at all times, even the middle of the night. One woman turned up at 12.30am, asking for a particular drug. 'Old missioner's wife took the same drugs,' she said; she'd run out.

Among my many tasks I was determined to change aspects of club life. I wasn't, like my predecessor, prepared to drink in the pub next door. He'd follow his 'flock' to keep an eye on twice-weekly socials. I wasn't interested; their behaviour was not my responsibility. The change was significant – bringing with it a sense of uncertainty, but I could not diffuse community tensions; I didn't have the ability, the knowledge of local deaf culture or the language skills. When a movement against me gathered pace, the ring leader led everyone out of the mission to a pub a quarter of a mile away. To counter such subordination, I wrote a banning letter and delivered it to the man's house. Such 'strong missioner' action helped clear the air, so the members soon returned.

In two years of hard work, I found new and better paid jobs for many, increased the church congregation, improved club facilities, set up a cricket club and promoted greater self-organisation – with committees and travel providing liberal and liberating learning experiences.

A group trip to Majorca proved an eye opener. After finding the small hotel near Palma harbour, I interpreted for the group but, against expectations, did not join the general activities. They asked why. I was, I explained, not the leader, but there to help with information and organising what they wanted; strange behaviour for a superintendent. Coming back, I suggested to a customs officer at Manchester Airport that he should ask everyone his questions at the same time while I interpreted. I stood on a table and signed, asking if everyone had packed their own luggage or if they had tobacco, watches or expensive goods. I passed on the replies – about cheap presents. On the bus back to Oldham, bags were opened revealing watches, rings and stocks of cigarettes. I blamed poor interpreting. I didn't mind; I smoked then.

Oldham was delightful. People were so kind and generous. Deaf individuals, such as Roy Tidswell and Hope Travis, emerged to take on the ideas and become community leaders. The work was rewarding and I was gently practising new attitudes in a place that appeared open to change.

However, the problems of living on the premises and the arrival of our first child meant the prospect of a move, when it appeared, was most welcome. Jimmy Hudson, my old boss, was leaving Leeds and suggested I return. We would be nearer Jill's parents and the post had national standing, but we'd be worse off. Accommodation in Oldham was free, as was the car that friends called the 'mission Zephyr'. Despite this, I had no doubts. I was, I thought, ready for the big time. I was hugely excited – but remarkable naïve.

After nine years, I'd acquired a level of missionary zeal, language performance and attitude, a kind of 'noble obsession'. I had come to appreciate that each community where I worked had to be thought of as part of an extended family, one in which the members' needs were more important than my own. I remembered my interview with the Church Missionary Society. Deaf missions were very similar. To be 'a worker with the deaf', one's family had to take second place: Love the deaf and be loved by them. The obsession had to be overwhelming. The implications for family life were therefore considerable. I remember a typical missioner family child complaining that her home was not a home but an extension of the welfare office. I hope my home was not completely taken up with the 'cause', but I know my life was dominated by the obsession, seriously impinging on family and other relationships.

I was often accused of being very defensive, even aggressive, but there seemed to be a need to defend deaf people and their culture. The criticism was that I was irrational, yet the insularity, conservatism and apparent selfishness of the deaf community had to be refuted. I was the one who knew, I was the one who was devoted and who cared. I felt that defenceless people needed defending; they were vulnerable and could be manipulated. If anyone was going to criticise, it was me because I was the one who lived the life and had acquired some of the secrets.

The required devotion constantly interfered with family life. The family had to live the missioner's life. They attended special church services, Christmas, Easter, Bishops' visits; whenever being seen as supportive was all-important. Institutional life allotted less time at home at the weekends than for others. Our family lived against the backdrop that deaf people were precious and special, even though this had been foisted upon them.

Problems facing clergy spouses and families are well documented. My children were not immune. I hope they can forgive me. It was all totally unnecessary. They may not agree, but I think the setting helped them become good communicators and with a good grounding in the protestant work ethic.

The chance to experiment and find strategies to change how deaf people thought about themselves was driving me professionally. Returning to Leeds would present an ideal opportunity to put undeveloped ideas into operation, even though my ideas about system changes were not fully conceived, probably more liked half baked. I was ready to start the 'real' job – in Leeds – where the missioner would take another quarter century to vanish.

5

Return to Yorkshire

Do not follow where the path may lead ...
Go instead where there is no path and leave a trail ...
Epitaph for Allan Hayhurst
(of the British Deaf and Dumb Association)

O N JULY 1, 1966, l was appointed superintendent of the deaf department of the Leeds Incorporated Institution for the Blind and the Deaf and Dumb, aged just twenty-nine and, after nine years, with at least reasonable signing skills for someone not from a deaf background. The task had three main components: providing a professional social work service for nearly seven hundred registered deaf people under an agency agreement with Leeds City Council's Social Services Department, meeting the needs of thousands more who were hard of hearing and thirdly, running one of the UK's largest and most active organisations for deaf people.

Since qualifying and leaving the city five years earlier, l had discovered how rural Cheshire and North Wales contrasted greatly with urban Oldham. Apart from practising skills learnt in training, l had had time to reflect on different aspects of the work. Deaf people living in, say, Snowdonia had deeply isolated and lonely lives. Deaf people from middle-class families living outside the influence of deaf communities seemed under most pressure because of the social and educational expectations thrust upon them. They had nowhere to acquire the collective wisdom and the experience of how other deaf people coped with their deafness. I had been able to spend time researching deaf people and their incarceration in mental hospitals and in Oldham, I had been able to test out ideas about promoting independence. The experience of these two very different organisations was invaluable.

Nearly a decade had flown by since I first made my way to the red neon DEAF sign and stood in the entrance hall of 135 Albion Street. Then, I looked anxiously into that imposing mirror on the left. Now I looked at the familiar blackboard, stairs and dark entrance passage. I was to meet Jimmy Hudson and his wife Mary, to have an induction – lasting just one day. Other staff appeared too, including the lady welfare officer with whom I worked previously and trainee Alan Haythornthwaite. Alan was seventeen and came from a deaf family. His brother Roland had just been appointed to my old job in Oldham, showing just how cosy the closeted deaf community was.

I cannot remember much about the induction other than the finance and bookkeeping. I really needed a week. Mary Hudson had a run a post office and was ferociously accurate with the accounts. Maths and money had always been problem areas for me so old anxieties quickly reappeared; I had to pretend I understood. Finance, particularly savings, was to take up much time. In place, and also part of my responsibility, was a branch of the Leeds and District Work People's Hospital Fund and a lodge of the Church Benefit Society. Many deaf people had accounts with the Leeds and Holbeck Building Society and their savings books were kept in the office. This not only promoted the north's traditional savings ethos but providing safekeeping for the books meant deaf people had to come to the office for money, so further promoting dependency.

I was handed keys to the two safes holding the petty cash and account books. A big roll top desk, which could be swiftly closed against prying eyes, held confidential information. It seemed a bold statement of importance, having been installed by AW Taylor in the mid-1930s. Like my immediate predecessor, Taylor had become a legendary national figure, running the Leeds institute for thirty-one years. Jimmy Hudson served for sixteen. I had come into a world that had seen little change for nearly half a century. The induction was a shock and my mind went blank. I could not think through or collate what was going on. I knew the lady worker made home and hospital visits while the trainee did interpreting and sport as well as now driving a minibus as a taxi service for the less mobile. I knew the weekly timetable and how it should be allocated. By mid-afternoon I was on my own.

Even before I had returned to Leeds, my thinking had changed, to become more radical and positive. I no longer believed in the attitudes that had been applied to the social management of deaf people for the previous hundred years. I wanted to change how deaf people saw themselves, to promote independence and self-awareness and help create pathways to self-care. I had also developed very strong views on the systems dominating deaf children's education. These had, in my opinion, failed. Nothing else was available, but a better alternative had to be found. I realised I had to work myself out of a job. I had decided this before the job interview but said nothing then or for a long time afterwards. I had no strategy, just a belief that I had been taught nothing ever likely to change the status of deaf people. With these lofty ideals I embarked on what became the main part of my career. I had no idea of the time this would take or the dramas that would have to be faced. Apart from which, I had more immediate problems to solve.

On the second day I was in the office early when a very anxious woman burst in. Her fifteen-year-old daughter had run away from home and was reportedly in a police station in Blackpool. The mother wanted to go to collect her daughter – and who better to provide transport than the new superintendent with a car. I drove to Blackpool and collected the daughter, who thought the whole episode very funny. Trying to explain that it was not my job to return a child to its parents (the council children's department had that responsibility) would have been complicated. Arranging transport, directions and an interpreter in Lancashire would also have taken too long for a distraught, weeping mother. So my first task had been totally, old missioner style – to do the expected and solve the problem. This wasn't, I thought, the ideal way to creating a new approach; it maintained the traditional pragmatism that glossed over any attempt to tackle institutionalised dependency.

By the mid-1960s, deaf people were showing some signs of trying to find independence, but not locally. Their identity remained rooted in being 'done to' rather than 'doing'. Allan Hayhurst of the British Deaf and Dumb Association was the only person I remember addressing the need for deaf people to become self-governing. He was a beacon. No one had any templates to follow. Some talked but little action followed. I had to find a way to accelerate the process. I stupidly chose words.

Years before I had seen on the hallway blackboard, the words 'Look what your Superintendent has done for you'. I replaced that with the slogan 'Don't come to me if you can do it for yourself'. Words were a mystery and feared by most deaf people. The office was regularly full of those carrying bits of paper bearing messages they could not understand. The shot was a long one into the future – and opposition rapidly emerged.

When I made my first public appearance for the organisation, the chairman announced that my predecessor, Jimmy Hudson, was always available if I failed. I think he sensed disquiet even that quickly. It was clear he had been told how different my attitude appeared to be. I was paid to help, so what was I really saying? It was certainly not the traditionally expected, unconditional acceptance of total responsibility for people's welfare. However, more immediate problems engulfed me, physically and emotionally, delaying any serious attempts at change. I soon felt swamped by the range of demands – and was totally unprepared and under-skilled when one particular aspect of the work reached me.

Late one night during that first week, the telephone rang. The police had deaf people in the cells and needed an interpreter. Years earlier, as a trainee, with insufficient interpreting skills, I had never appreciated the demands made by the police. However, they now had my phone number, as did the city's hospitals; I was effectively on call twenty-four hours a day, seven days a week, without any respite. So, for six years, I had to respond and interpret at any time. If someone was bailed, I had to take them home; that's what the missioner did. The car was supplied by the organisation and seen as part of the service.

If a deaf person was being questioned, statements had to be taken. This was a Catch-22 dilemma; by taking evidence from anyone accused or suspected, I became a witness to that information. If the statement went on to be questioned by lawyers, or became 'case critical', I found myself being the prosecution's chief witness; giving evidence against people for whom I was paid to care. Only one person was available for the work: me. I was locked into each case, trying to help both the police and a deaf person simultaneously.

Often a deaf person would be kept in custody overnight before appearing in court. After a night at a police station, usually Millgarth near Leeds Market or the Town Hall Bridewell, the missioner had to be back a few hours later, as sole interpreter for prosecution and defence. I had to negotiate with the police about what happened, a responsibility demanding considerable mutual trust. Officers liked getting rid of problems they considered trivial. The deaf person was pleased to go home and the missioner had pleased all the various interests relying on him. Deaf people were usually allowed bail during criminal proceedings as defence lawyers argued that the double isolation of detention and deafness was too severe. Historically, this work had been carried out without question. Documents record the Leeds missioner interpreting in crown courts at the start of the twentieth century. He, like me, was also called on by police in the West Riding and North Yorkshire, where interpreting services were few and far between.

I took a while to realise that dealing with crime, especially when alcohol or mental illness were also involved, was the most time consuming – and also the most stressful and disruptive to sleep and family life. I even had to break a holiday in Devon to return to interpret a murder case on demand. On average, I was called out twice a week to attend incidents ranging from fights and knifings to rape. Invariably alcohol was involved.

I identified the cause as a group of men who drank together on Tuesday and Saturday evenings. They gathered in the deaf club, where no alcohol was allowed, before going drinking in the city centre where they'd become violent and cause affrays. The group included pimps, thieves and others with a natural antagonism towards hearing people. Not probably a gang per se, but about twenty men would get themselves into danger. The hair on the back of my neck would rise whenever I found out they were in the club. I could sense something would happen but was powerless to prevent it. They were tough and several had criminal records and even managed to get all deaf people banned from one city centre pub. Being seen and standing firm were important; the missioner's status had to be maintained.

The violence was not always deliberate. There were some genuine misunderstandings. Once, a deaf person outside a pub witnessed a fight between the police and some people who had been thrown out. He picked up an officer's helmet but could not hear others' whistles. Failing to react quickly, he was the last to leave the scene and the first to be arrested; he had still been holding the helmet when reinforcements arrived. Despite going to help him, he was still fined. Similarly, when a deaf man's route across a road to reach his wife was blocked by a protest march, he could see her getting angry. He became impatient and raised two fingers to the marchers. He was arrested for abusing the protesters and their cause. Despite telling the magistrates what had happened, he was fined too.

Many situations clearly reflected such attitudes and the relationships between the missioner and the deaf clients. When one deaf person was held at Chapeltown Police Station, he was furious that I, the 'welfare', was not prepared to fight the police on his behalf. In contrast, I once found myself intervening between three officers hiding behind a counter in Millgarth Police Station and two deaf people trying to get at them. Waving my hands about, order was eventually restored so the deaf pair could be taken home without facing proceedings. This was hands-on work, rather than 'soft' welfare. The arrest of one young deaf man for theft brought the confusion and complexity of such work to the fore. The man already had a criminal record and appeared before the Recorder of Leeds. He could have gone to jail as he had pleaded guilty. After interpreting this and explaining the circumstances, the judge suddenly called me to the witness box – where he proceeded to ask me what I thought should happen. During that one case alone, I had four roles: on-call interpreter, expert witness, court interpreter and then social work manager for the defendant's rehabilitation. I had no guidelines to follow. Everybody's needs seemed to be channelled through this single, very powerful, but taxing role.

Much time involved visiting courts and solicitors. Apart from affray and assaults, I was involved with cases of murder and grievous bodily harm. Each required defence and prosecution statements, social reports, interpreting for psychiatric reports, prison visits and appearances as a witness. The missioner was also expected to provide support and rehabilitation. With confidentiality essential in such a close community, explaining my absence from the office and the organisation to other deaf people who wanted my help was difficult.

The workload was, however, reduced after a particularly high-profile murder in 1970 demanded huge time and energy. My relationship with the deaf community was not helped when one newspaper reported that I was 'helping the police with their enquiries'. I was grilled by Geoffrey Baker QC, for the defence. He examined my skills and ability and created practical tests, with the help of my predecessor, to assess my understanding of sign language. This took more than an hour and the atmosphere in the court was electric. He asked me if I thought I was a sign language expert. I said I was unsure of idiomatic sign language, particularly Glaswegian, which was why I had to be so careful. The court accepted the veracity of my interpreting and the deaf person received a life sentence. His family filled the public gallery; they blamed me for the fate of their son and nephew as they had seen me give evidence against him. As I had interpreted his own statement, a confession, I became a witness – the chief prosecution witness. Afterwards, I had to go to the cells to explain the sentence to the man, as well as helping the prison authorities. For several years, two men from the family followed me everywhere, which was spooky but understandable. Several years later, a marriage of convenience was arranged to try to get the life sentence reduced on compassionate grounds. The tabloid newspapers found out – and paid for the bride and bridesmaids to have shiny hot pants for the occasion. When I arrived at Wakefield registry office to interpret, I found the surrounding streets full of police, security and drama. For all the effort, the ploy failed. Five years later, the marriage was reportedly dissolved – as it hadn't been consummated.

The court work had one long-term advantage; I established better relationships with most of those involved than with any others in the deaf community. I rarely failed to turn up to deal with crises, spending more time with such individuals and learning more of their language. Adjusting to all the different language forms took time. I understood the dominant finger spellers but I found the rich non-English BSL difficult. I nodded and smiled more and probably made more mistakes – but I couldn't take risks in court. Whenever I could, I went over the evidence in advance, repeatedly. My thoroughness was however thwarted by one man, often in trouble with the police. He had a note which he would produce from his pocket saying 'I do not understand the interpreter'. Written by a friend he had made in jail previously, he would produce it whenever an interpreter was called in.

During the six years between 1966 and 1972, I was called to crown, magistrates' and coroners' courts, as well as various tribunals, more than six hundred and fifty times. One incident involved the transport authority, representing a man appealing against a ruling that deaf people could not be employed as drivers. We won. Each case was specialised and challenging, but made the nature and settings of my work continually varied. The experience, however, let me get to know many police officers, court officials, probation service and the lawyers. I used Victor Zermansky's practice – the lawyers there showed me how to approach legal problems openly and without pretention. I defied the committee's instruction to spread the legal work around various law firms; they did not, and could never, understand the enormous pressures; having only one practice involved kept everything as simple and straight-forward as possible. I was better known in the courts than anywhere else, but no one paid the organisation for this.

Many thought that such court work was my entire job whereas, in reality, it was officially only an adjunct. Nevertheless, it dominated my work. Having other obligations as well as this, I faced seventy-hour weeks of institute activities and social work, which included clinics – on Tuesday evenings, in the morning and evening on Saturdays and on Sunday evenings after church. I also conducted these services and wrote the sermons. Once a month I also interpreted holy communion for a visiting priest and, at St Anne's Cathedral, a Roman Catholic benediction.

Each month I had to write reports for the deaf department committee. Writing was still tortuous but my salvation was my secretary, Mavis Hawes. I had first met Mavis when she was ten or eleven. She acquired 'native' sign language from her deaf parents who brought her to social events when she was a child. I got to know her, even teaching her to dance. Her mother, Gladys, had helped me acquire some basic communication. Being around the organisation, she knew what went on and she allowed me to dictate my draft reports onto tape, greatly lessening the anxiety around my monthly appearances before the committee. She even exceeded her duties by helping deaf clients, before eventually leaving to become a social worker. Nearly fifty years later she told me that as no decent typewriter had been provided when she first started she had had to buy her own.

Committee members were concerned about the quality of life for their deaf people, so my reports named all those who had found work each month. Leeds expected its deaf people to work, so finding jobs was another important and time-consuming task for the organisation, even though the demand for semi-skilled men and women meant it was not difficult. As much of my court work was confidential, the committee never appreciated the extent of the commitment or involvement. The reports had historically named those convicted and their sentences, but after a time, I stopped this. I thought it inappropriate and the courts were then covered well by the area's newspapers. Instead I began writing more philosophically about community development and education. I referred to more general trends and the need for the organisation to consider its role. Depriving them of emotional titillation unsettled some committee members.

The newspaper crime reports confirmed the organisation's value – and as no one on the council payroll had suitable qualifications to work with deaf people, they relied on me to liaise with others, including the media. At first, I found dealing with radio reporters and television producers exciting and interesting. However, over time, I became increasingly frustrated by the superficiality and even ended up asking one broadcaster never to contact me again.

The committee consisted mostly of conservative lay people, but also included representatives from the local authority, as funders, assistant directors and elected councillors. Some were very aware and helpful; deputy directors of social services such as Margaret Howe and Jack Anderson provided sound advice and when Councillor Martin Dodgson appeared he became crucial to the organisation's future. Another councillor, Jean Searle, provided support too. Both our fathers had worked together rebuilding Plymouth after the war. Despite political differences, we spoke the same Devonian language. I considered the council my employer and talked to the officers as much as I could.

Each annual local authority grant was based on the previous year's returns. I found these to be inaccurate and, over time, had gradually to reduce some numbers while persuading the officials to accept new categories of those I felt the organisation should serve. The chairman of the organisation, Horace Buist, remained suspicious. He had been involved for years and knew the organisation's previous staff. However, I did eventually join the main management committee of the organisation and, with the support of the treasurer, local bank manager Bill Beveridge, I started trying to change attitudes. He accepted my financial inability and my ambitions, becoming a friend who saw me through much of the travail to come.

This continuing workload left me little time to consider my underlying aims and objectives. Major innovation would have to wait, but I had found some areas I thought I could influence. The first was to review life for deaf people in 'secure settings'.

Despite being away for five years, the deaf people I had visited each month during my training were still in High Royds Hospital at Menston. I thought three of them did not have to be there. Dennis Davies, the hospital's youngest deaf resident, showed no signs of mental illness. He was friendly and intelligent and I could never find out why he had been sectioned fourteen years earlier. When the Albion Street caretaker, Mr Darville, retired, I gave Dennis the job. The community welcomed him and helped him settle in. He stayed for many years. Then, one morning, he came to see me. He was leaving, he said, getting married and moving away. That was the best outcome I could imagine. The two others, older women, also left High Royds, and enjoyed coming to the 'centre' as I was now calling the institution.

I had also phoned Meanwood Park Hospital's medical superintendent, Dr Spencer, soon after getting back to ask if I could repeat my Denbighshire research. I would review everyone in the 'villas', as they called the wards then, whom the staff considered deaf.

I'd been prevented from visiting Meanwood Park hospital during my training either because the inmates were thought too grotesque for an innocent from the south, or for fear that I may discover 'difficult information' from the past. Unsurprisingly, I found some who shouldn't have been there. Geoffrey Abbot was a prime example. He had been sectioned twenty-two years before, when he was sixteen and, reportedly, difficult and aggressive. He had been consigned to Meanwood while his parents kept a more docile sibling with learning disabilities at home. Geoffrey was loved and contributed greatly to hospital life. He made himself useful, making tea, cleaning cars and the

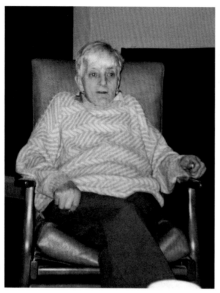

Geoffrey
Abbot

villa floors. The staff did not want him to go and getting him out took several years. His return to community life was supported by a new staff member, Roger Armstrong, but the institutionalisation lived on in him. If the pressure became too much, Geoffrey would get distressed and return to the hospital gates. Friends he had made at school had wondered what had happened when he disappeared. They were among those who rejoiced and welcomed him again when he returned to us. He was found work and tried to make up for lost time. As a forty-four-year-old, he bought a skate board, fell off and broke his arm. After that, the centre became his focus. He would come in every day, acting as an informal door man, welcoming people into the building.

I tried many ways to change the organisation's Dickensian atmosphere, but not always successfully. Brightening some areas with colourful paint caused some alarm. Such typical middle-class do-gooder efforts, like renting modern pictures from the art gallery and collecting flowers from the crematorium to cheer the place up, were not always appreciated. When I asked one deaf person what he thought of a Jean de Buffet painting he felt the frame and said he thought it was 'two-ply'. It was. Traditional expectations of the missioner's wife had also stayed in place, obliging Jill to continue making buns for each Tuesday's Derby and Joan Club tea party.

The missioner had always chaired the city's branch of the British Deaf and Dumb Association. I refused. Others thought me lazy, not realising my intention; creating opportunities for deaf people to make the organisation their own. A few people did come and take advantage of the new opportunities. Harry Ledger took over ironing the snooker tables; Miles Waterhouse started showing the monthly films, pleased to work the projector. John Lee began to clean the communion plate and organise the wine while Elizabeth Nichols started helping at the Tuesday afternoon teas, tacitly encouraging others to become more involved. Until then, keeping such tasks in-house had maintained the approach of 'caring welfare'. For me, each small change was a move in the right direction.

The centre's sporting activities flourished – with two football teams, cricket and swimming and other indoor sports for men and women. The inter-institute events, together with national football and drama competitions, helped provide full social lives for hundreds.

Indoor sports team in the late 1960s
Back: Laurie Goodall, myself, George Barker, Walter Chapman, Harry Ledger
Front: Helen Pemberton, Margaret Waterhouse, Yetta Custin, Agnes Barker, Barbara Keech

Football matches against teams from Glasgow were especially significant – as 'top town' rivalry came to the fore. The games themselves were very physical and, afterwards, local pubs did a lively trade. Fighting too was involved. There was always a punch up at the back of the club between the best fighters of both cities, with southpaw Albert Dixon representing the Leeds deaf interests. I withdrew, feeling this was not a place for the missioner. I closed the building, went home, and hoped the phone would not ring.

The long hours and consequent stress eventually took their toll. One day, after six years, I came to a dramatic halt, on the stairs in Woolworths. I could not move. Fortunately, Jill was with me and got me home. I stayed in bed for three weeks. I knew I could not continue working the seventy hours a week or more expected by the deaf people and the management committee, even though my original terms of service stated: 'Hours of work: As required. This is a welfare service'. I ignored a letter from the chairman saying I should consider my position if I couldn't fulfil my obligations. My doctor's conclusion that I couldn't continue the pace helped my recovery. Perhaps fortunately, this breakdown came at the same time as the call-outs decreased. The courts had started to impose longer prison sentences so the area's more active deaf criminals were behind bars and the telephone rang less often. The experience, however, helped me identify the core problem facing me and the work. I had to negotiate between a committee that provided and a community which expected to receive. I had to try to meet the conflicting expectations with an acceptable or deserving face. That could not continue. The non-developmental status quo could not be maintained.

Help came from an unlikely direction. It presented its own demands, on time and energy: moving. The Albion Street building was compulsorily purchased in the early 1970s, so a move provided the opportunity for not only a new environment but for attitudes to progress too. This defining moment signified the demolition of an old building and old attitudes and their replacement with slowly more enlightened attitudes towards caring.

In 1965, the Harold Wilson's Labour government had appointed Frederic Seebohm to review how local authorities ran various social services. The Seebohm report was published three years later, in July 1968. The recommendations, with an emphasis on supporting care in the community, included combining many local authority functions – such as welfare, home helps, mental health and social work – into single departments. Legislation requiring councils to implement many of the recommendations was passed in 1972, with significant implications for organisations such as ours.

I faced the simultaneous challenges of this and moving. I also knew that, if I got the strategy right, I could enable deaf people to see themselves and their places in society more positively. My thinking might have been arrogant and, paradoxically, authoritarian, but the underlying ethos was becoming more acceptable and, in light of the legislative changes, politically necessary. At the heart of this, I felt, I had to change how the community regarded missioners and how missioners saw their communities. In Leeds, the missioner controlled almost every aspect of deaf people's lives as they were centred on the building. For them, the conflicting aspects of fear, love, dependency and supervision would be withdrawn; for some these were replaced by distrust, dislike and contempt. Stepping away from the traditional, all-inclusive, 'caring' role was threatening – as enabling took over.

Family life would improve too. The first six years back in Leeds had been dominated by deaf people and their immediate needs. Holidays and weekends were often interrupted. By 1972 we had two children who were also expected to attend various functions. I came to regret how such intrusion affected us and know that nothing can make up for the losses. I will be forever grateful to Jill for accepting the situation and taking on extra responsibilities when I was absent at work. I could foresee change, a slow change, as I worked fewer hours. First though, the right moves had to be made.

6

A Chance for Change

THE STURDY BUT COMPLEX VICTORIAN building at 135 Albion Street in Leeds had housed the activities for deaf people since 1878. With the merging of the Institution for the Blind with the Yorkshire Association for the Deaf and Dumb, the building was a manifestation of a partnership much encouraged by the city fathers. Even so, blind people's needs – and services – were considered paramount. Catering for the needs of those blinded during the First World War led to an expansion into premises on Roundhay Road, with workshops and social facilities, in the early 1920s. There, the men made brushes, baskets and maps while the women, sometimes wives, knitted cardigans and socks. This independence lasted until 1938, when the organisation relinquished social and employment services for blind people, handing over the buildings, workshops, offices and halls to the local authority on a peppercorn rent.

When I first arrived in 1957, very little had changed for decades. The building and activities were very much the same as they had been eighty years earlier. The management structure had not changed either. The 1913 constitution stipulated that elected trustees owned the building. Responsible for running the organisation, they elected – or re-elected – a chairman each year.

At that time, one trustee was blind. They did form a deaf department sub-committee to oversee services for deaf people. By the early 1970s, it still was typical of the time, run with very little influence from its client group, despite having been properly managed and becoming well respected in Leeds. The deaf department committee remained the lesser priority until the 1948 National Assistance Act allowed local authorities to make grants. Deaf people were not represented in Leeds although some hard-of-hearing people did become involved. (This was deliberate – as deaf people were thought unable to be trusted with confidential reports that then included much personal and intimate information.) So, at the end of the 1940s and into the 1950s, this committee became responsible for effectively managing the evolving local authority agency agreement and annual grant. Each year, the chairman attended a council meeting to justify the funding which, in 1957 when I first arrived, had reached about £3,000. As department superintendent, I had a seat on the deaf sub-committee, but not on the main management committee. To get there, I had to earn my place.

Despite losing most of its responsibilities for the blind before the Second World War, the organisation still believed it was important in blind people's lives. They were considered more important than deaf people as their disability was more grievous. Making individual grants, paid for by the organisation's own resources, helped maintain this conviction. Often, as I left at the end of the deaf sub-committee meetings, I would walk past a group of home teachers for the blind, waiting to make requests to the management committee for anything from new radios to redecorating a home. The organisation did little more than this for blind people, other than support weekly tea parties around the city and a Christmas party.

The Albion Street building was central and easy to reach, on foot or by bus, but exceedingly inconvenient for older people or anyone using a wheelchair. Each week, the superintendent had to carry the chairs and their users up two flights of stairs to the main social rooms. More stairs and dim lights made parts of the building inaccessible. The building did, nevertheless, have its history, steeped in deaf culture and tradition. It fulfilled the needs of those who felt shunned and excluded from everyday hearing experience. People had played out their lives there, going as teenage school leavers, meeting future spouses, bringing their children, worshipping and playing indoor sports. Young deaf people used it as a base from which to explore other social worlds. They gathered there, became confident as a group and ventured out to pubs and dance halls. A grey lady reportedly haunted the top rooms while stories of suicide, fights and sex on the snooker tables were part of the rich tapestry imprinted into people's imagination. For many deaf people, it was their whole and vitally important life experience.

The impact of the commercially-driven compulsory purchase order on this ancient and precious human setting was immense. The users had not been consulted or informed until the sale of the premises was agreed. The trustees owned and managed the site and could – and did – do what they wanted with it. The announcement was met with anger and confusion, especially as I had not been told enough to be able to answer questions from the deaf community. Fortunately, they didn't blame me for what was happening.

Time was too short to think about a permanent alternative; we had to find temporary accommodation. Personally, I was delighted, welcoming the opportunity for change. The developers, Tarmac Northern, were keen to get on with the demolition. I said we could not, obviously, move until we had somewhere to go. I specified what was required, even as a temporary measure. Tarmac Northern's chief agent, Bill Dudley, helped find a site nearby. Acceptable wooden buildings went up and he promised, unofficially, a new permanent building at cost. The office block erected on Albion Street, named Dudley House as a tribute after his sudden death, has become K2 apartments.

The wooden huts, Belgrave Street, 1972-75

The temporary premises, three hundred yards away opposite one of Leeds' first synagogues, were ideal. They had most of the Albion Street facilities but were much smaller and all on one floor. I felt two displaced tribes were fittingly close together.

The huts also served my community development ambitions well, allowing people both to 'find themselves' and acquire a different collective identity. However, the circumstances left me no choice but to be authoritarian. Only one person could direct what was happening; no one else was available or able to make decisions and no committees existed with whom I could discuss the move. I also hoped my dictats would be the last instances of 'missioner knows best'.

A first change came with moving the contents of the Albion Street building. I told the users they would have to do this, giving them responsibility for setting up their new home. The volunteers, mainly from the church congregation, heaved much of the kitchen, furniture, desks and other equipment across the busy roads to Cross Belgrave Street.

With a group of deaf people that included Kelvin Pulman and Alan Dickinson, I watched and photographed the moments as the building was demolished and nearly a hundred years of intense activity and memories were razed. The façade came down to reveal the old name – Institution for the Indigent Deaf Mutes. While others were emotional, I knew I had to be positive, leaving much buried in the rubble, symbols of the past.

The new home – once established – would become the setting for great creativity. Although I hadn't written anything down, I had formulated my plans. I was determined to remove the power and authority of the superintendents-missioners, devolving six main areas of work to the community themselves or to the properly responsible statutory bodies. The first, making deaf people central in the organisation of their own lives, had started with the move. Other aspects of the centre's work would, as circumstances allowed, be manoeuvred into the remit of statutory agencies, with further education a priority. In the long term, I wanted to change the methods used to teach deaf children. Both Catholics and Anglicans would be encouraged to appoint qualified priests to administer spiritual services. Advocacy and awareness would become local authority responsibilities. Interpreting would become separate and distinct, away from social work. Job finding (placement) would be covered by the Department of Employment, leaving only social work, paid for by the council under the agency arrangement, to be the principle remit of our new Centre for Deaf People.

Although Leeds City Council could have ended the agency agreement at this time, the then social services director, Derek James, left it in place. He provided vital support as I began reorganising the professional services we continued to run. The change in local authority responsibilities had its ramifications. Many colleagues around the country left the voluntary sector as their organisations lost their agency agreements and the voluntary movement for deaf people in the UK began a long demise. I could have joined them, becoming a council social worker, but I knew I would lose any freedom for innovation. Deaf people would, I felt, be better served if these essential elements, so influential in their lives, were run properly by the various professional bodies. I would try to achieve each objective when I could. Such critical decisions, made by one person, unsurprisingly caused unrest and unhappiness, and if I had appreciated such ramifications, I probably wouldn't have gone ahead – and life would have been much easier.

The centre's temporary home was put together quickly and inexpensively as the community made the place their own. The end of the largest room was curtained off as a church area, with the huge, incongruous, painting of Christ, with his arms out of proportion, from the old building reduced to a portrait to fit. The lectern and other original artefacts, bearing the organisation's founders' names and dates on brass plates, went onto a low platform. Two, of the three, snooker tables were reconstructed. The canteen cookers and serving tables were put into position. Curtains were hung. The offices were more open and the absence of stairs made access easier for older people and those in wheelchairs. When everything felt ready, I asked the oldest and probably best-loved deaf person in Leeds, a woman called Annie Walworth, to perform the official opening – by cutting a ribbon.

A deaf person opening the new building was deliberately symbolic, demonstrating a new status and role for deaf people. I invited the chairman – and used the occasion to reveal some of my plans.

So, with that, deaf participation really started. The new environment helped concentrate thoughts and actions. We all stood shoulder to shoulder. The layout meant no one could hide. People could get at you – and they did. For some, the change was disturbing. The one element crucial to this was to form committees where debate could lead to action. In the six years between my return and the move, the deaf users had refused to form their own social committee. Organising activities was part of my job. The British Deaf and Dumb Association (BDDA) branch was the UK's largest, with four hundred members. That had a committee which I chaired. They refused to have anybody else but the move changed opinions. Calling on the 'sod him, we'll do it ourselves' principle of community development, I resigned, leaving them to get on with it.

By the time of the official opening, some committees were already working. However, my notice inviting volunteers to form a general committee remained blank for weeks. Desperate to relate more to those whose lives were changing, I turned to these other committees for representatives. Eventually, they came together – from the church, the indoor games teams, the football and cricket teams, the Darby and Joan club and the BDDA branch. I chaired the first meeting but quickly ducked out. This was not going to be my role; the missioner had to start vanishing.

As I hoped, the new home turned out to be a really good opportunity for changing attitudes and practice. Much, physical and intellectual, had been left in Albion Street. Now I had to get rid of the idea that I was totally responsible for the temporary building. I wasn't worried that the building might have collapsed; it was only a stop-gap. More important was establishing collective responsibility. I gave keys to those who were interested and left at 9.30pm instead of locking up myself, half an hour later. Instead of going home, I hid nearby and watched. Lo and behold, the building was made secure. The social committee, as it was now called, were taking charge. Activities flourished in the more intimate setting, attitudes to the organisation changed and people in the community enjoyed new powers.

A few people who had been personal acolytes of the old regime were, however, very distressed and angry; they did not want change. I could do little to help them and they became confirmed enemies. They demonstrated their dislike publicly and nationally, with serious consequences for what reputation I had. They were prominent and powerful in major deaf organisations, but similar issues were being confronted by the new National Union of the Deaf. Although Leeds was only part of this evolution, the process was far from pleasant.

Within two years the temporary building had served its purpose. Community development was under way with the committees becoming stronger and the main committee meeting regularly. Finding another, permanent home was vital. The management committee looked at several potential buildings before asking me if the disused public dispensary on North Street would be suitable. The former 39,500 sq ft hospital site did have restrictions on its use, but a voluntary social care organisation would be appropriate. Not far from the wooden huts, and slightly less central, the price was relatively cheap.

I knew I had to plan for a wide range of interests and activities. One day I sat on a bench, looking at the huge building across the

Centenary House

inner ring road. The imposing structure had housed accident and emergency services, clinics and minor operations. For thousands in Leeds, it was an historic place of care. I was enthused by the prospect of real innovation offered by its three main floors and considerable surrounding space. My plan emerged – for each floor to have specific and distinct activities.

The first level would serve the thousands of hearing impaired people in the Leeds area, offering aids and adaptations, information, advice and a counselling service; anything that supported deaf people without obliging them to get involved in deaf culture. They could collect what they needed to sustain lifestyles of their choice. The second floor would house traditional deaf services, such as professional social workers, meeting halls, stages for drama, refreshment facilities, further education and lip reading rooms that were part of the statutory service paid for by the local authority. The biggest change would, I envisaged, be the third floor. Deaf people would be encouraged to run the large area themselves, developing their independence, but without council funds; finance would also be their responsibility. The organisation's planning committee accepted the proposal, buying the dispensary in 1975.

The first task I faced, with caretaker Leslie Pickersgill, was going through each floor with strong disinfectant, buckets and shovels, getting rid of detritus left by tramps, squatters and dogs during the three years the building had been empty. Not joyful, but we got to know the building and made it our own. As we worked in the dark and damp, I paused to feel if any strange influences were lurking. I felt none. I had always felt I was being watched inside the old Albion Street edifice, perhaps by the collective spirit of my five previous incumbents sensing change in the air. As for the grey lady, she never reappeared.

When the architects and builders moved in, I began working with a few volunteers on one specific area – for the newly-formed Leeds Deaf Social Club. The chair, Evindra Lorenzo, described it well. It would, he said, be like a working men's club, but 'with women equal'. The committee's call for a bar met with expressions of disgust from a conservative clique. Historically, deaf people had not been encouraged to drink and the traditional thinkers saw this as a thin edge of a wedge.

Building working party

More volunteers, including skilled deaf people such as joiners, bricklayers and plasterers appeared each weekend to fashion a modern club setting. About fifty of them, men and women, worked for nothing. Walls were knocked down, welders welded, sewers sewed. For the first time, deaf people were making their own space.

I had to be very careful not to 'tell' people what to do too much. As soon as I could, I let other staff take over nudging the community through the demanding process of learning to run a social club. Tom Keegan stood out among them. He had joined us as a trainee social worker but dedicated himself to helping deaf people convert the top floor into two bars, a cafeteria and social facilities, personally raising over £10,000, mainly through events at the city's Belle Isle Working Men's Club where he worked part-time as a drummer. Later awarded an MBE, Tom and his colleagues were new and without my historical baggage. They communicated well and, with endless dedication, enabled the volunteers and the centre to develop.

The Deaf Social Club took off, quickly attracting more than four hundred paying members, both deaf and hearing. I chose not to go to the club unless invited, becoming invisible in the centre's social life. Instead, I oversaw the liaison between the main committee and the building's users. Copious amounts of beer were consumed, but in-house and without friction. The self-control further reduced the number of emergency calls to incidents in the city centre.

Other staff did voluntary work too, letting the missioner's work and influence diminish slowly. One committee member, Colin Bond, became active in the club. He was the first in the organisation's history to learn sign language. The management committee also changed. Councillor Martin Dodgson had become chairman of the organisation when Horace Buist stepped down after forty years. Martin was committed to the new approach. Under his leadership deaf people were, for the first time, appointed to both the management and deaf committees. His support was particularly strong during a year as Lord Mayor and he went on to play a key role in changing the policy towards education. Horace maintained his interest. Initially, deeply suspicious of me and my ideas, he eventually became a warm and supportive friend. He was right to be concerned, but delighted in the actual changes. With pride and sorrow, I gave the eulogy at his funeral. His family contributed to a new youth club.

This was all part of my strategy to destroy the missioner's role. Personally, I was winning but, because I had not told the committee enough, I was losing their confidence. In contrast however, the council's social services department did appreciate the issues, giving me unfailing professional and personal support. They realised that new staff and more training were vital for the moves, first from Albion Street to Cross Belgrave Street and then to Centenary House. They had paid for professional education, with assistant directors Margaret Howe and then Jack Anderson getting me to provide the arguments necessary to justify the expenditure. Without the staff in place first, nothing else would happen.

Prince Philip, the Duke of Edinburgh officially opened the building on February 13, 1976. Forthright as ever, he quashed opposition to the bar, saying he would raise the matter with the council if they didn't issue a licence. With deaf family members (his mother, Princess Alice of Battenberg, was born deaf), Prince Philip used signs naturally. The occasion seemed to mark the completion of a first stage of the transformation.

I interpret for Prince Philip in the opening ceremony

Prince Philip talks to curtain makers

Prince Philip with members of the Deaf Social Club

7

New Perspectives

IN 1966, IN ADDITION TO myself, the organisation had just two other employees, although a fourth, my secretary Mavis, soon joined us. One of the two was a highly-experienced woman, the other was a young man, Alan, with deaf parents. His upbringing meant that he was very knowledgeable about deaf language and culture and, at seventeen, his communication skills outshone mine. However, he felt very insecure with me in charge, aware that I did not share his background and cultural appreciation and left soon after my return. I called on the tradition of my earlier years in Leeds, finding people with deaf parents to undertake welfare work. The RNID said children of deaf adults (CoDAs) were best for such tasks. Sign language learned from their parents was valued but not, as circumstances changed, enough in itself. None of them stayed long. Despite my good will, I think I was, for them, an anomaly, not really part of the deaf world.

Growing professionalism also demanded higher standards and graduate qualifications. The opening of the first college of deaf welfare in London under the direction of established social scientists such as Professor Hilary Rose and Richard Titmus, had boosted the importance of social work. Consequently, our staff also needed the skills and knowledge crucial to reflect the increasing status of local authority social work – and justify the larger budgets. Bringing in graduates would also challenge stereotypical attitudes. I was relieved when the council agreed to let us include degree-level qualifications in our recruitment requirements and I also hoped the newcomers would accelerate changes in the missioner's role.

This professional training began while the moves were taking place. Roger Armstrong was our first graduate trainee, quickly followed by Christine Dunne who energised the youth club when she took responsibility for young people. Both were sent to York University on full pay for the two-year MPhil social work course. Council officials were horrified that a small voluntary organisation had done this, but when Roger and Chris returned they brought with them information vital to other new staff with only voluntary work experience. One, John Conway, was the first deaf person with deaf schooling to join the organisation. With natural sign language skills, he also became a resource point for the rest of the team.

The following twenty years saw far more people go on university courses. Each returned with different ideas and valuable attitudes, but more than anything, they brought much needed options and choices to the centre's users and clients. At any one time, the staff could offer deaf people a range of skills. Specialisms were developed in youth work, mental health and family issues. Hard-of-hearing people became more important, with aids and adaptations becoming a feature of the service. As overall manager, I deliberately encouraged personal interests rather than a traditional collective attitude to the individual and the community. Offering a range of people as interpreters was also important. Deaf people could choose from men or women, a variety of ages, backgrounds and sexual orientation. This was totally new, but I saw it as a means of increasing choice, many years before interpreters became distinct from social workers.

This approach had the underlying concept that everything was experiential. I felt that the established social work practice around deaf people was fundamentally flawed. New interventions, rooted in university thinking and governed by political dictats, were very different from the established practice and also very confusing for people accustomed to old-fashioned methods. However, the collision of new people, new attitudes, new buildings, new demands and new behaviour demanded such a flexible approach. This was working on the edge; it had to be if out-dated traditions were to be conquered.

As a group, our new social work staff did not appreciate what was happening. Away training, they had placements with local authority social services departments with safe systems that followed nationally accepted response patterns to requests for help. They returned to very different circumstances. Some of the traditional deaf background workers considered me unconventional in the extreme; the atmosphere was frequently flavoured with uncertainty. The newly trained provoked the ferment and questioning I wanted. Rightly, they considered everything critically.

I realised I had failed to articulate my own central ideas about change and destroying the authoritarian role but at that time few examples of my aspirations were available. Change had not yet progressed far enough to provide the reflective experience needed to explain how or why century-old working practices should end. Examples did exist elsewhere of traditional systems being superseded by local authority services. Some councils had stopped paying voluntary organisations, transferring their staff to statutory posts, often without the negotiation necessary to protect communities' long-serving carers. Frequently such relationships between clients and carers had been mutually dependent, practically incestuous. They were replaced by anger and confusion. I knew I was trying to supplant old ways with new systems emanating from legislation and wanted to use this time to teach people how to make the most of such changes and benefits. I saw this as a chance to become more self-sufficient and widen one's view of life.

However, such a grandiose optimistic aim sparked major conflict, being seen by committee and staff as a lack of leadership. They thought I had no capacity properly to direct the entire organisation; they were right that I had no intention of playing the time-honoured role of missioner. So, for a while, I satisfied nobody. Deaf people drew up petitions for my removal. The management response was that I should return to the loving and caring actions that avoided conflict. Still unaware of my tacit intentions, they brought in an external consultant who allowed for proper debate with the social work team. The verbatim reports of their meetings with the consultant said everything about the ferment of the time and the future. I was delighted.

The period was exciting. The team had expanded to include John Conway, who had BSL as his first language, a young woman with a history of volunteer work and natural language skills, the two newly-qualified social workers, both with MPhils, and a highly intelligent ex-sheet metal worker, Tommy Keogan. We stayed together long enough to establish new standards and attitudes in deaf social work. We developed our own culture and identity. Today, those involved say they look back appreciatively on the opportunities and experience of such a hectic few years.

Deaf people probably found it very strange to be faced with what appeared to be bizarre behaviour. No ties, no suits, women in trousers, gay people and deaf staff. The advent of deaf staff, in particular, was pivotal. John's appointment provoked entrenched attitudes. At first nobody went to him. Deaf people wrote to the management committee asking how a deaf man could help them, especially if he could not use the phone. However, it was not long before his understanding of deaf language and culture became valued, even though some qualified social workers could still not appreciate the importance of his language skills. Linking sign language expertise to social work practice, and seeing the benefits accrue, took some time.

Not being able to use idiomatic sign language always constrained my social work duties and I realised I could not build the most effective working relationships without it. I had so often seen the genuine language being used but couldn't grasp it for myself. I wanted to reflect the bizarre, the incongruous and the brash parts of my personality, but that was completely beyond me, even though vulgarity was outlawed; I had to set the standards embodied in missioner speak. My word-based humour was beyond deaf people. They didn't know me so I wasn't surprised when one frustrated women yelled: 'Who the fuck are you?' teaching me another useful expression.

I got a break too. In 1978, after twelve years and establishing a professional social work team, a gap in the training and secondment programme appeared. I had had no formal training in twenty-two years and was longing to catch up with those with qualifications. The newly-qualified social workers spoke a language I did not fully understand, leaving me feeling at a distinct disadvantage. A social work degree would help. As the staff had been to York, I first applied there. I had to sit in a book-lined room to write an essay on concepts of administration in social work practice. With my long-term underlying fear of writing and particularly spelling, I froze. I stood no chance of acceptance. The essay was embarrassing, increasing my mental darkness.

Instead, I contacted Bradford University and spoke to senior lecturer and course tutor Geoffrey Pearson. He asked for an essay on some aspect of my work. I sent him three thousand words outlining the various developments. He called me for interview and I was offered a place on the MA course in advanced studies of social work and community work practice. Bradford University department of applied social studies was headed by Hilary Rose, who had experience of lecturing on a deaf studies course in London, while Geoffrey Pearson had experience of deaf people in Sheffield. Immediately, someone knew something of my background.

I thought I was ready to examine the literature on all aspects of deafness and to review social and community work practice against the background of my practical experience. When I looked at the book lists I realised I was far from ready. I explained this to the committee and told them I needed to leave work at the beginning of August to prepare. They kindly agreed and I read every day for two months, cunningly concentrating on books written by my future tutors. I began collecting social science jargon and getting to grips with the concepts. The language used by the social workers returning from their studies became clearer.

So, one sunny day in early October 1978 I found myself in a high rise block in central Bradford called Wardley House. This might not have been the spires of Oxford but it was the higher education for which I had longed. Nobody cared about spelling; the tutors were looking for an understanding of concepts and intellectual invention. Professor Hilary Rose was splendid. She liked to throw ideas and concepts into the air and see how they were received. I found this ideal as I was doing the same at work. Having used the expression 'living on the edge', this was it. Once I had explained my background, I could even bounce ideas off the staff and other students.

One great opportunity for this came when we were invited to talk about our work. I am told I talked for more than two hours, pouring out the ideas and actions of the previous years. One friend said my talk seemed cathartic. I certainly felt greatly relieved. I was secure as a student and quickly found like minds. My classmates were a grand bunch with very varied backgrounds. To my eternal gratitude, one of them, Ann Peaseland, a training officer from the Leeds social services, even helped me rewrite my first rejected essays. Together both staff and students could not have been more helpful. They were highly intelligent and their depth of knowledge encouraged me to learn more. The breadth of radical thinking was there for the taking and I was not going to miss it.

One course module concerned philosophy. Particularly relevant was thinking that helped shape modern social and community work practice. Lectures covered writers selected as representing European thinking. I quickly realised I was floundering and said so. Lecturer Bob Ashcroft stopped his prepared flow of ideas and, for an hour, provided a superb resumé of the history of philosophy, filling a personal academic void.

Other lecturers such as Jim Kincaid taught me about specific social work issues and how these repeated themselves in wider contexts. Nothing, he said, was new and deafness was not unique in its human travails. A backdrop to my previous work was being painted and helped my thinking to come together. Studying organisations and their clients was also pertinent. This taught me that although I was working in a small organisation, its features and processes were well-known and that the frictions within the workplace had been replicated many times. I realised I was not alone.

I found one idea in Geoffrey Pearson's book *The Deviant Imagination* very valuable. He cited American academic Robert A Scott who wrote *The Making of Blind Me; A Study of Adult Socialization*. His hypothesis was a revelation. For years, I had tried to make sense of what happened to people who were deaf and here was the explanation. Scott explained how people are put through a socialisation process to a point where their condition can be managed. I borrowed the notion and, with great wordiness, devised a concept of socialisation producing a 'mature' condition of deafness. The hypothesis is also outlined in an Open University book, *Constructing Deafness*, edited by Susan Gregory and Gillian Hartley.

Spending time in a social work department was also very instructive. I expected ideas to be discussed professionally with change always on the agenda. Instead I found social workers could only concentrate on their everyday slog serving the state's needs for children in care and court actions.

The course took me though the emotional mangle caused by absorbing new philosophies that challenged strongly held beliefs. The smell of anarchy and revolution engulfed me and I lived an intense student life with a new language, new people and widening horizons. The entire process was so powerful that home life was seriously affected. I began talking another language called 'social work speak'.

Jalna Hanmer, my tutor, gave me unstinting support as I struggled to produce essays of the required standard. Passing four O levels had taken twenty attempts and was not the best preparation for a post-graduate course. I worked every day, apart from Christmas, from August until the end of the following May. With all the support from staff and students, and with considerable effort, I managed; it was deeply satisfying and the best professional year of my life.

I returned to work in September 1979 with the confidence of anyone newly-qualified – only to find total chaos. During my year away, my attitude towards development and experimentation combined with my lack of interest in administration had become more apparent and been exploited by staff. A stand-off between the committee and social work staff was not helped by letters from me, showing off my newly-acquired social work jargon. That did however do some good, as together with the broader appreciation of organisational behaviour that I had gained, I was better placed to appreciate the situation. It was clear: nothing in the organisation's life seemed settled. Such a predicament was disturbing, but also useful – as it was obvious to everyone who looked that the missioner was not, and could not, ever be in charge of everything again. The traditional role had been consigned to history, gone forever. Admittedly, I had lost control of the building and some staff, but I still oversaw the social work team and the organisation's continuing development.

Questions continued to come a plenty – from the deaf communities and others using the building. They thought they saw weakness rather than a role that had to evolve with the times, especially as my strategy for this development remained unshared.

These anxieties took about two years to diminish but understandable distrust remained. I hadn't been back long when, one day, the vice chairman marched into my office and accused me of anarchy, ironically perhaps, as I had just been studying the concept. His stance was a sure sign to me that the organisation had started thinking about both its structure and its future role for deaf people.

8

Attacking Education

Taking on the deaf education establishment came only after my own experience had provided me with the necessary foundation and confidence. This was a sealed area that needed prizing open. The policies behind educational provision had not effectively been challenged by anyone, other than a few deaf people themselves, for many years. The prevailing philosophy, which advocated the use of lip reading and the development of speech, were easy ambitions to respect and high ideals difficult to attack. Only deaf people really knew the disastrous effect that slavishly following this 'oral system' had produced.

By 1979, I felt the time had come to return to common sense and use deaf experience as the motive for change. The missioner had traditionally been responsible for continuing education when deaf people left school. They needed far more than I, or any social worker, could offer. Not only did deaf children need radically different approaches but the provision for school leavers needed staffing and financing from education budgets rather than well-meaning support from social workers.

The change did happen. One hundred years of educational oppression for deaf people in Leeds was overturned – but doing so took six years. Apart from tackling the situation of deaf people in psychiatric institutions and secure settings, the venture was, I believe, the biggest in my career. I was attacking well-established systems, locally and nationally. The odds were daunting. Deaf people had to win. Failure would have destroyed any hope of change for decades.

In the early 1900s, schooling took place in dedicated settings. The profoundly deaf were taught separately from the partially deaf, but they were allowed to mix socially. Standards in most schools were very low. Studies were boring and repetitive. The failure to educate deaf children was hidden behind the apparent success of speech teaching for those who were partially deaf. These pupils were presented to examining bodies to show off their skills, strengthening the 'correctness' of the oral philosophy. This may seem hugely critical, but deaf people have told many stories about being brought to the front of classes when inspectors visited. Two partially deaf men, John Smith of Pudsey and Johnny Longden of Horsforth, had hilarious stories about school life. John Smith said he was always presented to the examiners because he had speech, even before he went to school. Johnny Longden liked the deaf school because he learned to sign and could therefore talk to deaf people; his speech skills later took him into the army and a career as a driver.

Experience had influenced my thinking. It had started when I first began working with deaf people in 1957. My introduction to the Leeds organisation and the community had included being sent to schools to see how deaf children were taught. My first such visit was to St John's at Boston Spa near Leeds. It was, by national standards, good, run and taught with Catholic dedication – and a very strict oral system. No signing was allowed in class, despite a clandestine sign culture amongst the children. I went into a class of ten-year-olds, sitting in a semicircle, wearing huge headphones and looking like creatures from space. Miss Smith, an enthusiastic and kindly woman in her sixties was trying to communicate with amplified sound, blasting her way into their minds. She introduced me as 'Mr Smith'. One boy, who could speak, asked: 'Your father, Miss?' I was twenty and stood there helpless. A few minutes later, in the playground, when I saw some children covertly signing, I tried to make some contact.

The second visit was to Elmete Hall School. As the latest successor to Leeds' first school for deaf children, founded in the mid-1880s, in new, leafy lane, accommodation, the regime was less intense but the no signing rule still applied. I watched one girl receiving one-to-one teaching. She sat on a low stool with a mouthing teacher towering above her. She looked frightened and my heart went out to her. When the teacher left for a moment, I signed to her. I knew who she was, so when we met again twenty years later, I had a chance to discuss the experience with her. We agreed it was etched deeply into both our minds. She still had no understandable speech, but had become a proud mother with electric sign language.

Neither school had any teachers with sign language skills. Many years passed before a partially deaf woman was employed at St John's, where she became an icon for many deaf girls. After that, many more years passed before Leeds' teachers were obliged to learn how to sign. Such zeal reflected the missionary ferment of the moment; teaching methods that demanded 'these children must speak'. I had not questioned why, before the visits, Jimmy Hudson had warned me not to sign. However, I later discovered that my predecessor had been to Elmete School and had had the effrontery to sign to the children and criticise the staff for chastising the children with rulers if they signed, provoking a formal complaint. I took a while to learn just how common both physical and emotional repression against signing were at that time.

My third visit was to a special part-boarding school called Bridge House, at Harewood, north of Leeds, which took in deaf boys with perceived additional learning problems. Methods were similar – but for one significant difference: the children were considered so handicapped that signing, the language of failure, was acceptable and allowed. There, the boys, probably from the basic human necessity to communicate, had created their own signing culture. It was enriched because some came from deaf families where this was firmly established. The teachers learned from the children but without formal role models. Unfortunately, one housefather who could communicate well was later dismissed for abuse and I had to interpret during the subsequent police investigation. When I was in training I started going there on Sunday mornings to take the church services, held in a disused chapel about half a mile away. As it had been wired for sound, I spoke and signed, appreciating not only the experience but having the bus fares paid and lunches provided.

Years passed before the pervasive abuse and humiliation common in deaf schools, particularly boarding and residential schools, became public. The language that sustained their community and its life was subject to widespread contempt and ridicule. One school in Bradford made children stand isolated in corridors if they signed. Elsewhere, parents of deaf children were told not to use their hands as this would deter speech. This was, I felt distinctly inhuman – and inhumane. I began to wonder if this represented a covert understanding between the educational establishment and the missions. We didn't criticise, especially as their failures justified part of our existence and work.

Further insight had come during my five years away from Leeds. The double isolation of deafness and geography made those in North Wales even more vulnerable, especially to social instability as they had nowhere to meet and interact with peers from whom they could absorb lessons essential to life and living. Some defied the conventions. Oldham was an example. The headmaster of the school there, Alan Sherliker, was wise enough to adopt a more liberal regime while appearing to toe the party line. Even so, more widely in and around Cheshire, educational standards were poor, so deaf adults required explanations about written information. With this came a dependency, tying them into mission culture – and confirming that the standards had been too poor for decades. Class had an apparent affect too. Middle-class children face enough pressures to achieve and this was exacerbated for deaf children because the additional pressure disturbed them emotionally. Often, I had no choice but to confront parents who had been strongly advised not to use, let alone endorse, any sign language.

My time with both deaf children and deaf school leavers provided me with personal direct evidence of the shortcomings of this approach to their education. My unease grew when I also realised just how few deaf people had even partial literacy skills. Such attitudes can be traced to the Second International Conference on the Education of the Deaf, which took place in Milan in September 1880. Dominated by teachers who were not themselves deaf, the five-day event was so influential that signing was effectively banned from deaf education across Europe and the United States. The event quickly became infamous (in deaf terms), because the feelings, attitudes and experience of deaf people were ignored. The trend even saw children who could hear being put alongside deaf contemporaries in special schools – as if the teachers hoped that 'hearingness' would in some way be absorbed. (Perhaps most ironically of all, with hindsight, is that one of the two most prominent figures at the Milan conference was the inventor of the telephone, Alexander Graham Bell. A non-signing missionary, he was fervently against its use.)

Examples of alternatives shone, often through rareness alone. One was Edward Alfred Kirk, who was born in Doncaster in February 1855. When he was seven scarlet fever destroyed his hearing. He was admitted to the Yorkshire Institute for the Deaf and Dumb in 1866 but, despite good progress, left five years later. After being without work for a while, the then headmaster Charles Baker took him on as an assistant teacher – and his illustrious career began. Baker's successor James Howard followed Alexander Graham Bell's speech-only dogma. The consequent upset affected many, including Kirk. However, his prowess had been noted and, when a new deaf school opened in Leeds in January 1883, Kirk became its headmaster, the first deaf person to be offered such a job. He was still in post when he died in 1924. His triumph and dedication, during a period of concerted establishment opposition to having deaf teachers, is documented in a biography, *Leeds Beacon*, by Tony Boyce. Eight decades passed before Leeds appointed another deaf teacher.

The legacy of the Milan conference remained unchallenged for decades. The UK government's Department of Education had school inspectors ensuring those teaching the deaf conformed to its speech-only decrees while teacher training shunned sign language altogether. The chief course was at Manchester University, which did this so effectively that the academic in charge was knighted. Society, in its ignorance, applauded the intense effort being made to stop children growing up as 'deaf'; no other way seemed logical. In the early 1950s, cinema had contributed to the impact. In 1952, *Mandy*, a British feature film based on the novel *The Day is Ours* by Hilda Lewis, reinforced the apparent moral, ethical and social superiority of the tradition with a story of how a deaf girl learns to speak. Great stars of the time, Phyllis Calvert and James Mason, in leading roles implicitly added to its strength. The challenge to this by the short Oscar-winning film *The Silent Child*, produced in 2017 and causing its own stir, further confirmed the lingering power of the 1880 Milan conference.

Reality could not have been more different. Education was a profession of tacit but endemic failure. Most deaf children never achieved recognisable speech. If they failed to speak, or even try, they were considered deviant. Final school reports repeatedly used the word 'fail', implicitly blaming the child entirely. It took me some time to understand the methodology and grasp its consequences. Many deaf people told me they started adulthood feeling like failures. Over the years, examining two institutions at the centre of the ethos made the gravity of such emotions explicable. One of these was the teaching profession. The other was the RNID which, ironically perhaps, never really listened to deaf people. It never effectively opposed such failings, let alone debated them; there were only muffled mutterings from social workers, coinciding with growing anger and more radical movements among the deaf community.

Looking back, I think my personal childhood experience of dyslexia faced with the social and educational attitudes of the time provided me with the empathy necessary to understand such anger and frustration. The combination of personal experience and professional research underpinned my determination for change – but it took until October 1979, after twenty-two years' working life and, at last, the confidence of an

MA, before my stand as a total and vigorous opponent of existing deaf education became public.

My attempt to raise awareness of the issues around sign language had initially been covert after my return to Leeds in 1966. My onslaught, both political and practical, which started in 1979, took six years, covering seemingly disparate but nevertheless exciting and essential elements ranging from education for deaf people from Saudi Arabia, teaching sign language across Leeds and other educational initiatives, to embracing the evolving politics of disability and equal opportunities. What became a campaign emerged from a general aim and a rough framework boosted by good fortune and serendipity.

Eventually success came because teachers were too arrogant to believe change was possible. They had systems set in stone that eliminated any and every alternative. With few exceptions, they had also ignored developments around them for far too long. Such entrenchment also meant they refused to accept that a social agency could affect education.

PUBLIC MEETINGS

Annual general meetings provided an opening. Its original Victorian constitution obliged the organisation to hold an AGM each November when the Lord Mayor of Leeds would take the chair. Only subscribing members voted, as they paid the one guinea subscription stipulated in 1913 – way beyond what poorly paid deaf people could then afford. Apart from which, deaf people were not expected to pay for such services; after all, they were the objects of such charity. City patronage and council funding for work for the deaf effectively guaranteed the Lord Mayor's attendance, so this was therefore an ideal setting to start telling Leeds about deaf people and their need for sign language – as well as influencing the city's civic leaders. I invited powerful personalities from the signing world to speak. The meetings were interpreted so each Lord Mayor would see as many as two hundred deaf people avidly watching as their concerns were debated publicly.

Among those speakers was David Denton, the headmaster of a deaf school in Maryland. Despite the US influence in Milan, pragmatism had emerged over the decades, allowing a greater commitment to signing in the classroom. He was on a speaking tour of the UK supported by the British Deaf Association, whose deaf members fully endorsed his perspective.

Mary Brennan came too. She headed the Durham university department researching sign language. Her team established that, despite the education establishment ban, it was a genuine language, with its own grammar and syntax, as well as attributes that benefited its users enormously. As some of my committee members still regarded sign language as 'pidgin English', the impact of a well-respected academic obliterating their accepted and established attitudes could not be underestimated, even though the factions remained far apart for many more years.

Another AGM deeply appreciated the much-loved Dorothy – or Dot – Miles presenting her poetry in signed form, adding valuable credibility to deaf culture. Deaf people packed the hall and emotions ran high as her presence brought much pleasure and comfort.

Another US visitor was Harlan Lane, the eminent psychologist and linguist. He recounted his research into deaf discrimination and the battle in America for responsible education, both at and after school. He worked at Gallaudet in Washington DC, a university dedicated to deaf students named after Edward Miner Gallaudet, a staunch advocate of sign language. His book *When the Mind Hears* became a best seller and influenced politicians and planners in developed countries worldwide. His targets were the same as ours in Leeds.

James DeCaro did not have as far to travel. He was then working at Newcastle University with Professor Dennis Child, who later took over Leeds University's department of education. James' special interest had been training for technical employment skills at the Washington Technical Institute in the US. When he spoke of the possibilities of specialist training using American Sign Language as the method of communication, he exceeded our wildest dreams; that school leavers could use sign language to learn more.

When he came in the early 1980s, Stewart Simpson was head of the newly-created Council for the Advancement of Communication for Deaf People. He talked about setting up courses for sign language teachers and a register of interpreters, simultaneously acknowledging the need for a national response to deaf people's needs and that sign language was enduring. The demand for professional, qualified, interpreters was growing, presenting the incontestable question that if sign language had been banned by the education establishment for eighty years, why were interpreters in such great demand?

Each speaker brought a strong, personal perspective to aspects of signing to the council representatives, but one event did more than anything else to establish the language in the minds of council leaders. Martin Dodgson was the first councillor to become really involved with the organisation during my time in charge. When elected Lord Mayor, he welcomed the AGM to the Civic Hall banqueting chamber, providing a forum for emphasising sign language's value to the city's most influential figures. Innovation was to be the focus, reinforced by drama. Two approaches were put into competition. One was 'Total Communication'. This was created by Doncaster Deaf School headmaster Bob Dickson and senior colleague Cherry Grenville. They decided that the major independent school would use all forms of communication, promoting BSL, signed English, lip reading and speech together. The other approach was that used in Leeds – which excluded the use of BSL and signed English. One of the best new practitioners, Kath Gibson, came to interpret the meeting in BSL. As her parents were both deaf, BSL was Kath's first language. I was at the opposite side of the hall using the sign supported English that followed written word forms and adding clear lip patterns. We could both be seen clearly and amplification and loop systems were also in place.

We had deliberately posed the question: Which of us would the many deaf people there watch? Would they prefer the easy flow of the BSL or the rather stilted imitation of English? Within moments we could see that most of them were watching Kath's utterly natural rendition. The education committee chair, director of social services and professor of education absorbed the atmosphere. The deaf audience responded appropriately and immediately, breaking into spontaneous applause at the mention of John Conway, then newly-qualified and appointed as the city's first deaf social worker. The emotion was clear, passionate and significant. At the buffet afterwards, the informality showed how restricting means of communication had previously established and maintained barriers. The event boosted the status of deaf people, their language and the need for its use in education.

By this time, the campaign was building its own momentum. Others, particularly the parents of deaf children, contributed greatly as I sought to establish a platform for the language and its users. My objectives may still have been informal and unpublished, so they could not attract an official response which undoubtedly would have been negative. When one did come, it was too late. The impetus was, by then, too great to stop.

The Saudi experiment

An unexpected intervention from the Middle East also helped. Our organisation was not dedicated to education and did not have huge experience in such work, even though missioners had traditionally tried to support anyone wanting to go to night school with fairly random assistance. Consequently, in May 1981, a telephone call from officials in Saudi Arabia requesting a meeting about education was unexpected – and intriguing.

Days later, a delegation of four men in white gowns arrived in my office. They had an English educational adviser and were exploring training possibilities in the UK. They confessed that many deaf students in Saudi Arabia were failing – and that oral methods prevailed there, as in Leeds. I was delighted with the potential – explaining philosophies to them that had never been part of the thinking among those running Leeds education authority's hearing impaired department. They gave me a first opportunity to talk about how deaf people could learn successfully. Long deliberation had convinced me that deaf children should be allowed sign language as their principle means of communication. Unsurprisingly, I spoke at length and with great enthusiasm. I had written nothing down about my ideas on educational methods, nor could I point to any practical examples but I expounded my beliefs. Predictably perhaps, the delegation departed without comment. I heard nothing until July, when they wanted another meeting. They wanted my help and were ready to pay generously for various FE colleges' departments of continuing education to cover the subjects they required. We were asked to organise it all. I could not believe it.

I argued for an approach where the students would feel at home, immediately able to establish relationships with their support staff and the local community. This could only be done using the components of commonality, a culture that could only come from experiencing life among deaf people, living with them. To do this, I needed a team steeped in 'deaf experience'.

Opinions vary as to what constitutes deaf culture and common experience – but language is crucial. It is the conduit for social history from one generation to the next. Only then comes the sharing of visual perceptions of life and the community's collective knowledge and wisdom. The way the language is used – or performed – is central, not the signs themselves. Deaf people quickly diagnose deafness in others this way and within seconds of meeting me for the first time, a deaf person knows I am from a hearing background. It is something about being able to use the idiom of the deaf which they themselves recognise. Then there is the capacity to anticipate movement; recognising such a need without requiring words is core to the deaf psyche. Physicality – touching and hugging – is important too as is the initial interaction of signing when people meet. It determines whether the motivation exists to continue to negotiate in the language to reach a satisfactory mutual understanding.

I learned this in Nerja, a small Spanish community about fifty kilometres east of Málaga in Andalucia. When I was there in the 1980s, I met Manolo Villalon, a professional beggar, working tables of holidaymakers, handing out finger spelling cards and then coming back to collect any money. Profoundly deaf, he was educated by nuns and had strong sign language but no English and my Spanish is rudimentary. I tried to communicate using my hands. He responded, using a Chaplinesque mime. With a little effort from me, this intelligent and interested man learned that I came from Leeds and that the woman with me was Jill, my wife. Gradually, I convinced him that I didn't want to dominate the language form and he started teaching me his signs. I used them as we talked more and became friends. Later, he asked me to translate his Spanish sign language into English when he addressed meetings about the problems of deaf people in Spain. As we got to know one another, Manolo told me more about the repression he experienced from the nuns – while I noted the similarity with others' school lives in the UK. (What is it in the human psyche that needs to punish others for being different?)

Most deaf people have common experiences. Identifying them comes before the sharing and building on commonalities essential to learning. Consequently, when the Saudis arrived at Heathrow Airport, the first people they met had to be deaf, with a 'whole-life' understanding of sign language and deaf culture. I asked two excellent communicators, Terry Harton and John Smith, to go. Their involvement was fruitful. By the time the coach reached Leeds for a more formal reception, contact had been established and the visitors were relaxed. Our building became their 'deaf house' and home.

For once, I wasn't trying to change social perceptions with innovation, as I had been arrogantly doing with my social work perspective. This was education; the knowledge was there. All they needed was access to it – and that required the right team. I could set the criteria, so I brought in an expert signer, Peter Llewellyn Jones, deaf people themselves and those with deaf parents. I wanted a group who would make the Saudis feel comfortable, while Park Lane College in Leeds would select the technical teachers to work with the interpreters and students.

The Saudis settled in, using Centenary House as their base to enjoy new freedoms and experiences – despite the reservations of their authorities about the on-site bars. The support continued when they had breaks from studying. The budget allowed our staff to take time off and be paid to go away with the students on holidays as their interpreters. The students' rapid progress confirmed that the approach was realistic. Ironically, in a city where the mainstream education authority banned sign language for deaf people, we had direct evidence that deaf students could learn technical subjects using sign language. We had proved that education for deaf people based on a system that rejected entrenched philosophies and practice could succeed. I relaxed a little, letting the project stand for itself while acknowledging that if some of the students did not themselves speak, then their government's money certainly did talk.

When, after three years, the Saudis departed, having done far better than their predecessors had done in non-signing environments, some of the deaf people recruited as classroom assistants also had to go. Their lack of English meant they were less useful than when dealing with the Saudis. My desire that interpreters – and their assistants – should be college staff rather than ours meant I was also powerless to protect their jobs.

FURTHER EDUCATION AND SIGN LANGUAGE TEACHING

Coming back to Leeds in the mid-1960s, I found I was expected to teach at evening classes for deaf people. The students, usually between the ages of sixteen and twenty-five, came from the two local schools; Elmete Hall and St John's Boston Spa. I panicked and asked their teachers to take on the job. There was no response. I knew that the classes were a legacy from the early schools and mission days where the roles of teacher/social worker were often interchangeable. The work was obviously important and needed to be continued, so I had to get on with it alone. I did however find some support in a local junior school headmaster, Harold Curry. He might not have had much sign language but did help me teach both maths and English.

Although I had never taught before, the prospect excited me. I was paid extra too, which helped the family budget. When twelve people turned up, I started by assessing how much English they knew. They revealed that they had been bored by repetitive school work so, working from the assumption that if they were having fun, they'd stay, I asked them to set each week's topics – as the start of informal sign language discussions. What else could, I thought, be done so spontaneously? Not surprisingly, the teenagers were fascinated by the sexual slang they had met when starting work, always having been presented with medical terminology at school. My time in the Royal Navy again proved useful, as it had been where I'd encountered such language. And, for the first time, they were with teachers who could and would use sign language.

I also used the classes as a forum for another aspect of the missioner's work – introducing Christianity to the young. Enough started coming to church to make confirmation classes worthwhile. Getting close to people and moulding them into good institution members were indicators of success. I felt I was making progress with this, as it brought together all my previous experience. And, this particular extracurricular activity made a pleasant change from dealing with the weekly callout to deaf people who had become violent in Leeds pubs and streets.

By 1988, the local education authority had taken over the continuing education remit, establishing a dedicated continuing education team and new methods of teaching.

Even in the 1950s, the organisation had provided some sign language classes – for officers from Armley prison. They were taught to finger spell as, then, three deaf people were in the jail. A decade later I revived these sessions, even though they were rudimentary, teaching the manual alphabet and basic signs such as 'good morning' and 'good night'. Primitive and without any firm underlying method, the classes were nevertheless a start of some sort. In the 1960s I had nowhere to turn for help or advice. No organisations existed to provide this, although the research that later spurred teaching courses at Durham university had begun and the Council for the Advancement of Communication with Deaf people only came into being in 1982.

My first seven years in post allowed little if any opportunity for language learning innovation. My attempts to run non-verbal communication classes were seen as unprofessional, even though I wasn't trying to teach finger spelling but rather illustrate the core philosophy of signing by encouraging participants to forget about using words while trying to think about existence in terms of pictures and sensations. Those attending faced great difficulties, not least being asked to confront themselves as 'non-speakers', unable to do anything but produce pictures of themselves. One could not come to terms with this, another simply walked out, while others wanted to bend the signs into following English syntax. The methodology was very experimental, but interest grew as teachers and training centre workers sensed change in the air and wanted to be involved.

Our sign language classes, financed by the council, started in 1979. By 1985 we had expanded to eleven classes – all taught by deaf people the organisation had financially supported to go on the Durham university courses – and by 1992 there were thirty-one classes.

OTHER INITIATIVES

The advent of the Conservative government's Community Programme in 1982 provided another opportunity to promote sign language education in Leeds. The initiative, to provide young people with training at a time of great unemployment, meant councils had sufficient funds to create temporary jobs, with voluntary organisations bidding for money. We were among them – as many deaf people were without work.

We won funding to put a deaf person with good sign language beside an unemployed teacher or graduate to run 'deaf awareness' sessions. Groups, schools, building societies and government departments all took advantage of the free training. At last, deaf people had opportunities to teach their language and experience while simultaneously gaining from being with educated hearing people, some of whom also had teaching skills. They filled the centre – bringing their ideas with them. The initiative was so successful that eventually twelve people were involved and about fifty were trained during the lifetime of the Community Programme. Most ended up in education of some sort, either as teachers for the deaf or communication support workers. The deaf people themselves became support workers or worked in communication too. After working as an upholster, one deaf person said the experience was the best in his life. Another realised he was a natural carer, progressing into a fulfilling career in the mental health sector.

Another scheme saw a deaf person as foreman of a team of builders involved in building the Butterfly World attraction in Roundhay, Leeds.

When the government finally ended the programme in 1988 – it was too expensive – progress had been made and a demand created. Leeds City Council took over key projects with a department dedicated to running deaf awareness training for all new staff that was even extended to medical students at the city's teaching hospitals.

This period also further lessened the traditional role of missioner – especially by eliminating the link between promoting awareness and begging. I had achieved another goal. I could focus on other aspects of the organisation's increasing work.

SELF IMAGE

The rigidity of deaf people's attitudes towards themselves and their community was pervasive in the 1950s and 60s, appearing alarming with hindsight. Clear demarcation separated what they did and what they did not do. (The perception originated and prevailed for two factors, I believe. Firstly, deaf people were isolated by society. Then, secondly, they faced lives structured and constrained for the convenience of those who provided their education and social care.) The Community Programme also provided a chance to improve this self image.

By then, sign language was being promoted as belonging to deaf people, enhancing the pride of the deaf community. The programme funded a project that allowed us to take on a trainee photographer, Jon Crooks, so he could improve his skills. He would, the bid said, spend a year recording the centre's work, including every aspect of deaf life and activities. Within twelve months, his portfolio included pictures of parents and children wading through the trauma that society imposes on the deaf experience as well as images of people at work and play. From initial reticence in front of a camera, inhibitions disappeared – and the entrance hall walls became covered in prints.

An exhibition, tracing the development of early sign language in children to mature communication, was put together – and

This page and next - photographs by Jon Crooks, used in the exhibition

Kirsty Paterson

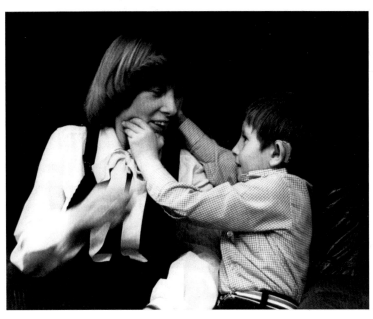

James

James joyfully demonstrates the 'banned' language

taken to Leeds' Grand Theatre to accompany a production of *Children of a Lesser God*, the Tony award winning play by Hesper Anderson and Mark Medoff that was made into a movie in 1986. This brilliant play highlights the conflict between the teaching of speech and the natural use of sign language.

I failed in my attempt to write a description of the language being portrayed; I could not find the words. The exhibition was displayed all round Leeds, further encouraging deaf people to be open about their condition and their language. The education controversy was also public, so images of a strong language and positive lives provided yet another crucial contribution towards further development.

I had come back from university in 1979 ready for a new challenge. I told the board that I intended trying to change the council's education policy. Fearful of the relationship with their funders, they advised caution, but did not stop me. I abandoned the years of covert innovation, aware that those who paid me now knew my views about deaf education and attitudes towards sign language.

Nothing changed immediately although both increasing sign language teaching and liaising with education officials were acknowledged and encouraged. Great encouragement came from a senior figure at one of the city's continuing education centres, Area 7, in the Hyde Park district of Leeds. Tony Evans could navigate council bureaucracy as well as writing strong proposals with realistic recommendations. Well-established continuing education, provided by part-time deaf teachers, coincided with increasingly popular concepts of equal opportunities, linked to equitable access to education. Together, these opened a route to establishing a professional education team at Centenary House that officially used sign language. Suddenly, the organisation was both politically correct and had some clout.

Our ideas attracted senior education officials who encouraged further innovation – including encouraging the establishment of a three-strong team to promote sign language. A co-ordinator would have overall responsibility for training and liaison while the two other staff would be involved with providing sign language in continuing education. After numerous meetings, lobbying councillors by inviting them to meet deaf people at Centenary House, and even besieging some in their offices, the funding was approved. I knew who would be best for the work and even wrote the job descriptions, but distanced myself from the selection process. Those I hoped for got the jobs and moved in. With this team in post, I could move on to focus on trying to change the wider policy around deaf children in mainstream education.

Education policy for those with special needs had attracted a greater public and political profile in the 1970s. In 1974, the educationalist Mary, later Baroness, Warnock had been appointed to review public policy. The report bearing her name was published four years later, underpinning the subsequent 1981 Education Act. The impetus was that deaf children should be integrated in mainstream schools. While independent establishments such as the deaf school in Doncaster and St John's at Boston Spa were excluded, by the mid-1980s Leeds council was contemplating closing Elmete Hall.

While numerous battles had been won, the war to change deaf education was not over. Leeds was the site of a final stand – when two lecturers from Manchester University's deaf education department were due to address the Leeds education committee – about a new aspect of their work, called 'natural oralism'. I feared the worst. The committee chairman, Councillor Geoff Driver, quickly agreed that deaf people should be invited to the meeting. Arrangements were made so an usher who could sign would direct them to specific seats together. Word of the meeting spread quickly once it reached Centenary House. The British Deaf Association provided interpreters, so the sixty deaf people who convened on January 31, 1985, could be totally involved. The lecturers were true to form, perpetuating the century-old tradition of excluding sign language in favour of their approach. After a break, the committee got ready for another breakthrough – hearing the views of deaf people themselves. No one endorsed the lecturers. Deaf people told of having no option but to go to Gallaudet University in the USA – where total communication was the foundation for teaching – to find higher education. The collective anger convinced the committee that change was imperative.

This defining moment was followed by lobbying from numerous individuals and organisations. A senior teacher and total communications devotee Richard Squires surveyed future needs. Richard had, with another teacher of the deaf, Clair Laye, started using sign language, in a school with a deaf unit, before total communication had been officially sanctioned in Leeds. I helped by collating sixty sets of papers on total communication, arranged by British Deaf Association education officer Susanne Turfus, for the committee. The politicians faced the difficulty of adding another change to a system already in flux. The acting head of Elmete Hall, a convinced non-signer, intervened, asking for the names of councillors we had lobbied. My refusal added to the tension because the newly-politicised deaf community was demanding change.

After a review called for by Councillor Driver, the committee decided in September 1986 to adopt total communication, overturning the wholly oral-only approach and ending the battle. The council also agreed to finance a unit at Leeds University to train teachers in the new skills. While acknowledging that lip reading was essential and speech important, the natural language of deaf people would no longer be an object of contempt or indicative of failure. This revolution also welcomed deaf people to the classroom. Frustratingly, since the death of Edward Kirk in the 1920s, the only deaf people employed in schools had usually worked in the kitchens, washing up.

I wrote the job description for the first head of the new service. Miranda Llewellyn Jones, who had previously run the then newly-established sign language team in adult education, got the job. Probably the UK's leading exponent of bilingual education, using oral and sign techniques, she was totally committed to our objectives. Her appointment allowed me to relinquish this campaign, although the Centenary House centre remained crucial, providing somewhere for trainee teachers to learn about deaf culture and the language. With earlier social boundaries consigned to history, they became increasingly visible in the social club and its life.

The organisation's youth club also became more important after Elmete Hall finally closed, providing a place for children to meet, while the teachers who had moved from the school to the city's special education needs department made their presence felt at an office in Meanwood. Additionally pleasing for me was the visible decrease in the dependency that typified young deaf people's attitudes under missioner regimes.

Despite the progress, regrets remained. Some deaf community leaders felt that the impact of the Warnock Report had ruined their prospects. I had to compromise too. I believe now, as then, that specialist schools, staffed by teachers totally immersed in deaf history and culture, would be the most effective way to educate deaf children.

Changes were also reflected in continuing education. My twelve night school students, desperate to learn, never became fully literate. They had started too late and one evening a week was definitely insufficient. Also I was no teacher, but a friendly communicator with then untested ideas. Twenty-five years later, however, I was delighted to see Leeds have its own sophisticated unit catering for school leavers' education. However, all this was still inadequate. Total communication had yet to enable deaf students to achieve as much as their hearing counterparts. Academic standards had improved and expectations changed, but still too few deaf students were getting to university.

Confirmation of our success came with royal approval with a visit from Diana, Princess of Wales in 1989, three years after Leeds' momentous and courageous policy change. The princess had become patron of the British Deaf Association and, as well as learning some sign language, was keen to find out more. The BDA told her Leeds was the place to see.

I had been on holiday when the call came from Kensington Palace. When I got back, we had just six weeks to prepare. Everyday life tends to stop for royal visits but we didn't want to do anything other than present our normal selves. Fearing negativity, the centre had never courted media attention, but we knew to expect an invasion and consequent scrutiny. We rejected thoughts of tidying the building; we would be warm, realistic, adventurous, challenging and supportive as well as, above all, being unstuffy and non-bureaucratic.

Those six weeks were extremely fraught. Centre users had to decide who to invite. Friends were lost and won before the lists were compiled and timetable agreed. The emphasis would be on work and sign language, with the princess using interpreters. She would go to a sign language class and experience the telecommunications facilities used by deaf people as well as meeting our various user groups.

Our rehearsal, like the best before any successful performance, ended in a shambles at 11pm the day before the visit. Despite the moans and groans we learned our lessons and were ready for the day ahead.

Winter lingered for that March 4. Leeds was overcast, snow blowing in a chill wind. For once, the building had been empty overnight, but it quickly filled well before the 10.50am press call. The board had decided that the day would belong to deaf people, not them. Friends came too, some even among the police security team and our own professional photographer, Jon Crooks, was on hand as well. Diana arrived ten minutes early, making her way through the crowds and, after brief formalities, met Hannah Walker, the city's oldest totally deaf and blind person, who had been using the organisation for more than sixty years. Their mutual delight communicated itself to everyone, setting the tone for the rest of the visit.

Seventy minutes later, revelling in the success, the party began in the centre, bringing together every age group for the first time. Deaf people had been at the forefront and Diana had responded, especially to the children, with obvious joy. A picture of her using finger spelling for her name appeared on the front page of the next day's *Daily Telegraph*. She told us she wished for a similar centre nearer Kensington Palace so she could visit more often. Sign language had royal endorsement; no one was going to tell Diana not to use her hands to communicate with deaf people.

Diana and me with sign language teachers Leslie Townend, Maureen Wood and Miles Waterhouse

Spelling D for Diana

Her visit may have been brief but it consolidated years of innovation for deaf people that were otherwise visible only to centre users. For example, I remember one quiet junior youth club evening when a five-year-old Indian girl appeared in the foyer, having lost her father somewhere in the building. She used the most exquisite sign language to ask a deaf adult if her father had been seen. 'What does he look like?' he asked. She had just provided a very detailed and accurate description when he appeared.

This incident is important because just five years earlier, deaf children were still discouraged from using the centre and parents were influenced to believe that signing would diminish communication between themselves and their children. Only if the child's parents had been deaf would the event have occurred. Witnessing such a normal, natural – and beautiful – piece of communication was fulfilling and joyful. I had no further need to attack education.

9

The Vanishing Act

WHEN I STARTED, MY WORK had five distinct aspects. By 1990 most had disappeared from the organisation's remit. That isn't to say that deaf people's needs had gone too; they had not, but they were being run by more suitable individuals and organisations. For us, only social work remained, as a personal service. The details of how those elements of work vanished from the missioner's remit concludes this story.

My efforts to change education policy had also, deliberately, removed teaching from the missioner's work. While those around me may have thought I was failing as attitudes and activities evolved, I felt I was winning as areas of work were transferred to government or local authority management.

I came to believe that interpreting for a deaf person, wherever it took place, was an intimate and highly responsible task. When I started, interpreting was not controlled by deaf people. Everyone expected missioners – who knew more than deaf people ever did – effectively to decide what was in anyone's best interests. Deaf people were often totally excluded from such conversations in a way that blind people and wheelchair users are often patronisingly overlooked. My conversion came when I was asked by Kelvin Pulman, a deaf person, to interpret when he went to the doctor.

He introduced me as just that, not by name, when we arrived together. I was a conduit, not an orchestrator. Rightly, I was constrained in that role. The occasion came several years into my career, when I was already having reservations about then current practice. I was relieved to function more appropriately and remain grateful to Kelvin for the opportunity.

When services expanded and more staff were employed, the deaf community had a chance to think about the suitability of interpreters. Should they be younger, older, gay or straight, male or female, black, Asian, Jewish or white? Such dilemmas came before professional, independent services came into existence.

Evindra Lorenzo

Leeds' first service emerged from a council consultation exercise. The centre's community liaison officer, Evindra Lorenzo, took me to many meetings to interpret for him. The experience prompted the belief that only a totally separate service would best serve deaf people. I felt it should be housed away from the main centre, Centenary House, as that would enhance confidentiality. Evindra and most deaf people wanted it closest to existing services. They won.

A council equal opportunities officer, Howard Beck, helped get the service going He had worked on our Community Programme scheme and when that finished, and the council took over the work, he moved over to council employment. To emphasise independence, interpreters had offices in Centenary House as far away from the social work team as the building would allow. Bringing it to life had taken thirty-five years but when that happened, it was properly overseen by a committee of users who monitored standards and professional ethics.

The mechanics of finding people work had been a significant activity, requiring specific skills and knowledge, but it was not one that the new breed of professionally qualified social workers considered significant. As employment training became more specialised and with the advent of youth employment services in local authorities, the state assumed these responsibilities. However, the links were not broken entirely – I was among those who helped train officers specially recruited by the Department of Employment to advise disabled people. I contributed to national courses run in Leeds for twelve years and then in Sheffield. When the course moved again, to Manchester, the RNID took over, adding greater professionalism. The introduction of the Disability Living Allowance (DLA) in 1992 seemed to lessen the political pressure forcing disabled people into work. Further legislative changes later increased employers' obligations to support disabled employees too.

Originally, running the organisation's social life took two people. A welfare assistant or trainee missioner organised the sports and social events for the deaf club while the missioner himself arranged holidays and outings for the older people. Leeds' eminence added running national competitions to the workload. Transferring these responsibilities to deaf people themselves took years. I grasped the opportunity when it presented itself, even though I again faced allegations of laziness and disinterest. No reasons had ever existed to prevent intelligent deaf people running such facilities themselves – other than the ethos of controlling them. In the social club paid cooks and stewards replaced social workers, who only went in for lunch or a drink after work. I kept my distance from the organisation's social life and felt totally justified in purging the previous practices.

The evolution of the religious dimension was significant too, moving from a focus on a deeply-involved individual missioner, present every Sunday, to deaf worshippers becoming part of a broader Anglicanism. I feel less happy in the way I broke away from providing spiritual care. The process was decidedly acrimonious and personally painful, when an almost total loss of faith took place. This coincided with my unstated aim of removing that historical missioner role.

The Church of England and the Roman Catholic Church are inescapably linked with deaf care. The earliest missions emanated from the nineteenth century philanthropy in which clergymen were also significant educators. Both denominations were convinced that deaf people needed spiritual guidance to become 'full' people. Speaking (English) was most important, not least because 'In the beginning was the word'.

The involvement was still strong more than a hundred years later – as the *British Deaf News* of June 1969 detailed ten organisations working with deaf people, seven of which were chaired by Anglican clergy.

Even in the 1950s, the Deaf Welfare Examination Board, responsible for training, was full of worthy clergymen striving to ensure that religious instruction, in schools and social welfare, continued. The annual courses I attended in the late 50s were held at the diocesan house in Sheffield, Whirlow Grange, but even then divisions between the religious and secular were apparent. The trainees came from larger deaf organisations and welfare agencies around the country. Some were clergy while more were just openly religious. Some went to evening prayer while others went out to night clubs.

Apart from these few days each year, my only instruction came from John Swain, who had moved to St Michael's in

Headingley from Cambridge. Together John and the courses met my spiritual needs then. I felt my work had a vocation and I did not question the approach to deaf people I was acquiring; the way their problems were managed was wholly compatible with this religiosity. Deaf people who took on the church's morals and ethics were the missions' essence and strength.

My first attempts at leading Sunday services, in 1957, were a struggle. Such travails, however, strengthened my conviction that I was in the right job; the pain was justification, of a kind. Religious thoughts and emotions took me over during those first few months, transporting me to a different, mystical world. By the first Easter I had – frighteningly and disturbingly – lost mental control. I had to keep such omnipotent passion in check. Religious work in Chester and north Wales was very much a token affair, but Oldham was very different. I applied to become a licensed reader while working there, but the local vicar turned me down; we disliked one another. I was confident in charge of the deaf centre and probably appeared to lack humility.

Returning to Leeds in 1966, I threw myself into church work again, becoming a lay reader soon afterwards. The sport, social work, placement tasks, interpreting and general contact were all times when I could try to exert influence for the good of the church. Sunday after Sunday I left my growing family to conduct services or interpret communion. Within a few years twenty-six deaf people were confirmed. A church council was formed with congregation members taking more part in the services.

The organisation expected me to do even more at Easter and Christmas, without extra pay. I had to lead and preach at services on Good Friday and Easter Sunday and arrange transport so the elderly and those in wheelchairs could get to Midnight Mass at St John's on New Briggate in Leeds city centre. For many years,

I didn't get home until 2.30am – after which I was still on call – and too often the police or hospitals needed help dealing with the festive fall-out.

The churchgoers may have been practising Christians but that did not embrace becoming more self-reliant or skills development. Sermons customarily reinforced perceptions of giving and receiving rather than preaching individual liberty. Unsurprisingly, some baulked when I did this, viewing such calls for change as a negation of duty and responsibility and becoming a sort of official opposition. Others, who appreciated my ideas, became friends.

The move to Centenary House let me encourage the deaf users to create both Catholic and Free Church chapels. I was determined to avert the antagonism between deaf Anglicans and Catholics that tarnished communities in Manchester, Liverpool and Glasgow. Questioned as a waste of space, the congregation was enthused by Father Eamon Cowan and the exertions of a professional joiner produced beautiful results that guaranteed its place. Although used less frequently than the other spaces, the services were well-attended.

My Anglican congregation included some who could follow my sign-supported English while others, who didn't, probably came only to enjoy the different, but nevertheless caring, atmosphere. Two years after the move, I tried to involve them more – by using BSL. Hearing Catholics and Anglicans had long been repressed by the clerical use of Latin. I viewed the move to BSL like abandoning Latin in favour of English. The attempt was met with horror and not appreciated. I like to think that if my signing had been better the offence would have been less, and I could have explained my motives. Nevertheless, I had again broken the unspoken rules. The formation of a church committee had been a first step towards appointing a chaplain to take over from the missioner; this had to happen if the old-fashioned post was to disappear. Again, I encouraged deaf people to participate more in the services as well as parish life. I interpreted when one deaf person from the committee started attending meetings at Leeds Parish Church, now Leeds Minster.

As well as influencing my professional practice, my year at university in the late 1970s brought together conflicting philosophies and other social work professionals, from very different backgrounds, and this affected me spiritually too. Many of my duties, including the church work, had been performed well by others while I was away. I let this continue, which allowed me more time at home. I recognised I was no longer appropriate to provide spiritual leadership or make such missioner decisions – even though the Church of England happily accepted my free services as a lay reader. Stepping down and handing back my licence allowed me to highlight the need for someone else to take over this responsibility. Even my children noticed I was more relaxed.

For several years, deaf members of the congregation led their own services with staff members as interpreters until Helen Begley arrived in Leeds. Although she had come as a 'hearing therapist', she was intent on the priesthood. Negotiations between the organisation and the diocese, headed by Martin Dodgson, eventually led to her appointment as chaplain to deaf people in Leeds – but only after her inclusion in the first ordination of women at Ripon Cathedral in late September 1989. I interpreted that service, relishing the fusion of feminism and the finale of my personal ministry. When Helen was inducted, the functioning missioner in me disappeared and the historic role was put to rest, hopefully for ever.

I remember once interpreting the annual service commemorating St John of Beverley, in East Yorkshire, as the patron saint of deaf people; the Minster there has a stained glass window depicting Jesus healing a deaf person with the command 'be open'. Another visit, several years later, provided a moment for reflection – thinking about my religious experience with deaf people and its conclusion. I had learned much about the various church organisations working with deaf people. I had confronted the beliefs and attitudes and I had witnessed change. My analysis revealed many questions but few, if any, answers. Had I just wanted to escape? Had I cleverly caused the role of missioner to implode? Had I wanted more family time?

I accepted the demise in the apparent power and dominion, feeling that I was stumbling towards anonymity. Others may have seen failure but, be it a happy accident or genuine guile, I felt my determination to see my intentions through to this close had been justified.

A STEP TOO FAR

The total evolution of the organisation was not, however, complete. I went to the committee proposing still further radical change. Their muted response suggested they didn't believe it was possible. By this time, even Centenary House was cumbersome and dated, as was the management of the twin remit of caring for both blind and deaf people. Staff numbers had increased from three to thirty-one. I foresaw a new structure, in a new building, free from historical baggage. I also believed I could convince the organisation to accept, to me at least, a further logical step in empowering the clients.

My proposal document said deaf and blind people should run more services themselves – as well as supporting the increasing number of ageing deaf and blind people on behalf of social services or the NHS. Existing services would continue, but with management changes.

Our choice of Allen Tod architects proved astute. We produced a powerful video showing deaf and blind people putting forward their ideas, valuing the forward thinking and adding more when they appreciated the underlying concepts. Meetings, even those with the city's development agency and official bodies, which Evindra Lorenzo and I attended, embodied the excitement of innovation and ferment of hope and expectation.

After the development agency found an ideal site, between the bus station and the city's theatres, the architects produced plans for a new home, as well for extending Centenary House as an alternative. The council leader saw the video and backed the scheme. A new building would shake off any lingering historic artefact and attitude, repeating more radically the effects of the moves after the Albion Street premises were demolished.

I relished the possibilities for expanding our collective thinking and cultural exchange. I saw a role for myself, with a whiff of self-importance. Four years after planning began, I presented the scheme to the board. I argued that we should sell Centenary House to cover half the cost and look to other sources for the remainder. I was greeted with silence – and heard nothing until the architects told me the development agency had been disappointed to learn the scheme would not go ahead. I had stupidly believed in the ideal. Without adequate comparisons, the risk had been considered too great. Later, the furious chairman raged at me, mightily. I had to accept that while the board had let me develop my ideas, they could not endorse an adventure that would have financially destroyed the organisation.

I might, if deaf community support had been guaranteed, have fought on. But the missioner's power, and mine with it, had gone. As I distanced myself from their activities, they had complained, alleging that I was aloof and disinterested. I could not have it both ways.

I felt my twenty-six-year involvement was ending and I needed a way out. It came when I got a visit from the assistant director of social services saying our budget was being cut by six per cent – about, I reckoned, my salary. Retirement beckoned. My departure on August 28, 1992 was very quiet, proving painfully for me then, that the missioner had truly vanished.

10

Freedoms and Frolics

MY FULL-TIME WORK ENDED with speeches – and generous gifts. Colleagues had been embarrassed as collecting money from the deaf community had proved difficult, but other groups using the centre, such as those for the deafblind and hard of hearing, were more forthcoming. I was not surprised. I had distanced myself from the social club to force the community to find sufficient strength to run its own affairs; action regarded as such disinterest that I ceased to exist, even though none of the services they received had been affected by my elimination of the missioner's authoritative role. Wine from the church congregation accompanied gifts from deaf individuals whom I had known for many years.

The day before my retirement had been traumatic. We were burgled at home – for the fourth time – probably because word was out about my retirement and the gifts were tempting. One, a bottle of champagne, was left behind on the doorstep.

I still felt accident prone a few days later. Jill and I had left my last 'do' to drive south. Our tour ended at the Salcombe Hill Hotel in Sidmouth. As I climbed the scrubbed white steps to the hotel entrance, I snagged a bag of golf clubs I was carrying. It held a bottle of claret, given by the church, which I was smuggling in to avoid paying bar prices. It fell out, smashed and spilt the red nectar all over the steps just as the proprietor was coming out to meet us.

The days in Devon passed quickly with old friends and family and we came back to a different life in Leeds, where I could control when I worked – if not always what I did. My pension arrangements were such that, even at fifty-five, I was precluded from working full-time. And, as Jill had been promoted to management, her hours were rigid and stressful. I wanted to get home before her each day and take over the cooking and shopping. I wanted variety too. I had enjoyed work most when the settings and responsibilities had fluctuated – from being in charge one moment to being a worker the next. In seven hours, I remembered, I could have four or five different roles.

I never really missed the work. That told me I'd left the organisation at the right moment. Between leaving and finding something new, I spent several days just sitting and looking round our front room, trying to visualise a world away from such intensity. I also realised how much I loved my home and its artefacts.

Despite this, I wasn't idle. I had been appointed a justice of the peace in 1990 and sat regularly on the magistrates' bench. I offered to do more, chairing family courts. I also considered doing more in education, as a communication support worker, interpreting in the classroom. I had, however, set my sights on a part-time MA course in deaf culture and sign language at Durham University. The two came together as I was asked to support a deaf teenager in a neighbouring authority and to do some hours in a Leeds school, shortly after I had been interviewed and accepted onto the Durham course. I had quickly become very busy.

The school 'lad' was huge, from West Indian origins, and a natural poet with a great sense of humour. I couldn't be professionally detached when with him; we enjoyed deaf humour and learning from one another. I was ready to interact with deaf people as myself, without the baggage of my career. He knew nothing of missioners, regarding me as simply useful and helpful as he questioned and learned, boosted by the apparent status of having this older bloke as his personal communicator.

Physically limited, he was frustrated at being denied the group sport his contemporaries enjoyed. I did however teach him to tackle – properly, if slowly – and how to run and pass the ball, while other boys were playing rugby or in the gym. He couldn't kick or jump but he could roll, so we invented a game of seeing who could roll most quickly from one end of a long mat to the other, taking turns to time ourselves. The others couldn't understand the laughter shared by a fifty-five-year-old white man and a fifteen-year-old black youth. What did we both find so funny?

My young client had to cope with the drastic transformation from being the subject of hostility to an object of curiosity. I had deliberately not intervened when he got involved in a one-sided and painful fight with another big lad. His classmates couldn't decide whether I was a teacher or an authority figure. I could see them watching us, taking a while to accept me. My presence seemed to add interest – and an expectation that something might happen – even though I had become a non-judgemental communicator with good intent. He wrote poetry full of raw emotion unfettered by any sensitive reviews of other people's feelings; what you got was so uncluttered.

Class time could be intense, especially when perceptions were being exchanged during history lessons. During a project about the First World War, I joined in, bringing in family postcards sent from the front to contribute to a discussion about the Battle of Verdun. The teacher really valued having an interpreter-friend while the pupils, never having seen such objects, seemed to wonder if I'd been among the fighting.

When the class was asked to imagine what it was like to be involved in the war, my client asked if he could write a poem, before turning to me and saying 'you write one'. Two very different poems resulted. I had to voice his from his sign language for them and interpret my words for him as I read. When I finished, he looked at me and said: 'You me different. Me inside look out. You outside look in.' His immediate reaction was stark and perceptive; his verse was hard felt and involved; mine was observed and more detached.

Despite being well accepted, I had to leave after three months as the education authority wanted someone full-time. Leaving was really painful, with the class producing kind cards and cartoons; I even had gifts from the staff. My client wrote poems that quickly became treasured possessions.

My new life had started with fun and excitement and an appropriate level of commitment. I enjoyed not being the boss and just helping the educational process. School hours were relatively short and left time for shopping and cooking.

I quickly, and importantly, realised I could never be a detached information conduit. I saw too much need in the students and the social worker in me would not go away. This was when the first interpreters were being trained, arriving in classrooms with professional rigidity to protect them from any involvement. No wonder then that further conflict wasn't far away.

I applied for permanent part-time work as a communicator at Bradford College. Five women interviewed me. They seemed concerned that I would not fit in, having had management experience. Why, they asked, did I want to work in education? I answered honestly and simply: classrooms excited me. I got the job and stayed with them for twelve years.

I started the Durham course at about the same time, enjoying the weekends with fellow students. The fun however did not last; serious personal difficulties intervened. When I was driving home in the evening after the second weekend, I ran into a violent snowstorm. I slowed down but soon realised I wasn't seeing or hearing any lorries until they were really close. I was so alarmed that I left the car a short distance from home and walked the rest of the way, despite the weather.

The sight in my right eye seemed blurred. The optician I saw said it was macular degeneration that goes with age. When the blurring continued, I realised this wasn't all. A specialist immediately diagnosed glaucoma and severe damage. Hospital visits and eye operations failed to stop me losing the sight of my right eye entirely – and much confidence. My hearing was also failing, and I needed aids for both ears. This wasn't good; so much was changing – and frightening. I needed time to adjust. Pouring wine, driving and moving round supermarkets all demanded different skills. Medical attitudes that monocular vision did not present appreciable difficulties upset me, although I had myself previously regarded partial sight and hearing as being lesser problems; a typical professional standpoint. I remembered my early working days – and the concepts of 'proper deaf and proper blind'. I had so much to learn and re-learn that I was motivated to initiate a monocular support group in Leeds.

Old friends said I was being punished for leaving work early. Ignoring them, I still felt unable to cope with the study, or travelling to Durham, so I reluctantly withdrew from the course. However, after about three months, and with support, I did return to lighter work at Bradford College. I found a slower routine – dealing with less academic subjects, such as tourism, leisure and catering, which taught me a lot and allowed me to adjust to having one eye. Cooking had become a passion and I took over the worktops and cooker at home to practise what I interpreted in the training kitchens.

I worked with one person studying clothing design who needed to learn new signs for specific work such as pleating. Lacking such experience, I turned to deaf friends in the trade and, from them, learned signs created over the decades, part of the cultural history of deaf people in Yorkshire's huge clothing industry.

From the outset in the classroom, I faced the dilemma of students' emotional needs. Hearing students would share their feelings before classes started, while their deaf colleagues were excluded, even though they also needed the insights and emotions of others to help them appreciate their own trials, turmoil and joy. I felt privileged, once they had confidence in me, that they said more. Some revealed abuse, cultural adjustment and, of course, affairs of the heart. At first, accounts of pain, frustrations and concerns that had built up, often over years, came as a deluge. Then, unburdened, learning came more easily. I could not turn my blind eye to this, so usually tried to arrive early so those who wanted to could come and chat.

Generally, I said nothing to my supervisors. In social work, confidentiality rules, especially in closed communities. Some disclosures were however so serious that, after discussion and agreement, routes to professional help were sought, putting me in conflict with colleagues who believed in greater detachment.

Language itself was evolving in Bradford too. The city's Asian deaf people were adopting their own different signs. I realised I still reflected the English dominance of missioner talk – so learning the local vernacular was a chance to shed even more historic baggage and find even greater personal freedom, even though I'd never be as fluent as a first language signer and hadn't been professionally trained to acceptable BSL standards. I once asked a good deaf friend what he thought of my signing, he said 'It's OK, it's Martin Smith talk'.

Enforced waiting during gaps between classes provided time for reading and thinking. I wrote more poetry and researched work ethics. I hoped for professional interest but found little response when I tried to start a debate comparing the work of communication support workers and teachers for the deaf.

Over the next few years I finally managed to change my own way of thinking about using language, abandoning words in favour of using emotion as expression. I enjoyed this new way of mixing with deaf people as it rekindled my childhood pleasure in acting. I wished more had been understood about the principles of sign language performance when I started work. No one then had written about the origins of sign language or how it worked as a first language. I had to discover this for myself and, despite asking frequently, no qualified interpreter ever explained it either.

While at Bradford, I also got to work with Terry Harton again. I'd known him all my working life, often running into each other professionally as well as sharing much of fifty years in the Leeds centre, the church and helping with the Saudi visit. Now retired, he'd come to the college to do a fine arts course. This was a splendid chance to spend time with a friend

Terry Harton

interpreting a subject of mutual interest. It also had its moments. For instance, I enjoyed interpreting the raciness of a session about the history of art and the media, standing beside the lecturer in front of about eighty students. When the lecturer asked which image the media never showed, only Terry's hand went up. 'Yes?' said the lecturer. The others were enthralled as I enunciated, with as much dignity as I could muster, Terry's response: 'The erect penis'. His answer was correct too.

Despite the pay being about as poor as for cleaners, I continued to find education exciting. It was always inspiring to go into an educational setting and my enthusiasm was rewarded with strong friendships and confidential information from staff who regarded me as a trusted outsider. The work could be stressful and demanding too. A year with an MA social studies student confirmed this. My more qualified interpreter colleagues found the jargon and concepts too difficult, so my own MA came to the rescue. The biggest challenge was the speed. I had to discuss much with the student during breaks or at lunchtime. Two five-hour days would leave me exhausted – but that individual did get his degree and went on to a nationally important position.

However exhausted I might be, I still found time for the magistracy, mentoring others in the family courts before taking on yet another new function – as chair of a health service complaints panel. This was a new role and I found it very different from my previous experiences. If I had had power before, it was because I was the most knowledgeable or experienced of those with whom I was involved. Here, I had to be both even-handed and in charge.

My first tribunal seemed daunting. I was so nervous that I damaged my car on the way there, but I was still first to arrive. In an enormous room, I found tables lined up with eight chairs on one side and one on the other, presumably for the complainant. I worked off some anxiety by moving the tables into a tight rectangle for me, the admin staff, two medical consultants as advisers, the doctor facing the complaint and the complainant, as a less daunting arrangement. The hearing was uneventful and there was general agreement on the outcomes, but I feared writing the report although by then computer spell-checking helped greatly.

Over time, I achieved decisions by consensus, allowing the complainants sufficient time to express themselves fully and calling adjournments if those less articulate became muddled in the hothouse created by highly communicative professionals. Distressingly, most cases could have been settled much earlier with appropriate apologies but medical arrogance still prevailed, making retractions rare. My favourite reaction came from a complainant who reported that the chairman had treated them 'rite nice'.

My own increasing deafness brought this nicely remunerative, and very responsible, work to an end. By 2000, I reckoned I missed a quarter of the words anyone said, and sometimes I could not spot the speaker if they were physically too far to my right. With monocular vision alone, I could probably have continued but I was becoming increasingly anxious about the two together. Having seen others struggle on, I wanted to avoid unnecessary mistakes. So, with regret, I stood down from both the tribunals and the bench.

Even then, I maintained my commitment as a communication support worker with its varying degrees of intensity, before I ended that when I reached seventy-one, unsung but having resolved, in one way or another the various communication dilemmas that bugged me throughout my full-time career. This was the time to swim, play golf, cook and care for my family.

The missioner had finally vanished.

My family - in 2007

Epilogue

Full Circle

RUNNING ANY SOCIAL SERVICE PRESENTS a continual conflict between finance and ethics for those in charge. The Leeds Society for Deaf and Blind People is no exception. However the first two decades of the twenty-first century saw that conflict become far more intense – with huge ramifications.

I left the organisation in 1992. Then, and for most of the following fifteen years, funding for the voluntary sector in England was relatively generous. Central government appeared to appreciate the social value of such organisations and their work. In Leeds, for example, this allowed my successor director to take over statutory responsibilities for the welfare of blind people for the first time since 1938. Consequently, the organisation and its services expanded.

The global financial collapse of 2008-09 took a huge toll across much of the voluntary sector. The irony was particularly acute in the UK. Conservative prime minister David Cameron was loudly advocating a 'big society', rooted in volunteering, at the same time as his chancellor, George Osborne, was implementing financial austerity policies depriving local government of the funds essential for such voluntary organisations to operate.

Councils had no option but to put welfare services out to competitive tender. Although some welcomed apparently greater professionalism, such commercialisation undermined the fundamental ethos of the sector. In the political turmoil and focus on other aspects of the financial and economic chaos, no one noticed; an essential aspect of UK society changed with hardly a whimper from the public.

As far as deaf people in Leeds were concerned, the organisation I had run for so many years was forced to bid to run the very services for which it had been established and of which those involved had decades of individual and collective experience. It failed to win the contract. Generations of wisdom and knowledge were sacrificed as officials decided that another organisation, from outside the city, could do the work more cheaply. Many other voluntary organisations, not just in Leeds, but around the country have suffered similar fates as they were forced into apparent money-saving mergers, laying off managers with years of experience and knowledge. The passion and compassion of those who had established such organisations, recognising the need and importance of close, local operations, were thrown on the bonfire of 'efficiency' vanities.

Austerity had a domino effect. Cuts to community education budgets eliminated the sign language classes that were once free. Premises have closed. Leeds once had thirty-one such classes – and a determination to become the 'signing centre of the north'; that fantastic opportunity fell by the wayside. The council was forced to abandon its requirement that every new recruit went through deaf awareness training, as did medical students, home helps and care workers. Such empathy, if not compassion, was deleted when job descriptions were rewritten. Experienced managers had enough of the changes and moved on, taking their dedication and wisdom with them. When generic 'business' managers appeared; the need for senior personnel to be fluent in sign language and imbued with the culture of deaf or blind people disappeared – with long-term consequences that are difficult, if not impossible to measure, and consequently cannot appear on anyone's accountability spreadsheet.

The appearance of more freelance interpreters has let agencies such as the Department of Employment hire such services as and when needed for the short-term, without sufficient consideration of the quality or long-term implications or relationships with individual deaf people.

The effect of the loss of the city council funding was that the traditional home of such services in Leeds – Centenary House – was all but abandoned. The social work was run from an impersonal office miles away. The 'one-stop shop' approach, with all its invisible and incalculable worth, was abandoned, apparently in the search for greater value for money. All that remained was the interpreting service, run by the society's administrators, paid for by the NHS. Unsurprisingly, all the other Centenary House activities collapsed – because no one was there to provide the essential informal support. Its social facilities closed and the sports events ceased. The chapel was stripped, although its religious trappings were rescued and put into storage. Deaf Catholics went to St Anne's Cathedral, asking me back to interpret for them until someone else was eventually found.

Predictably, deprived of a physical heart, the deaf community atrophied. The advent of the internet and electronic communication, that have otherwise greatly enhanced the lives of deaf people, were no substitute for personal, face-to-face interaction, even though they have reduced dependency on pubs as the adhesive of many, strong cultural bonds. In this context, the very existence of the organisation became uncertain. With so many individuals under greater financial pressure, volunteering per se became a burden for many; only the retired or financially stable could afford to give their time. Putting time and effort into running an organisation that was not apparently valued by the local community, through the council, seemed increasingly irrelevant to the board.

After nearly twenty years away, in around 2011, I was approached by some deaf individuals, a former director and other staff to help the organisation regain its focus. We found new director-trustees who quickly realised that the only option was to sell Centenary House and use the proceeds to buy smaller, more manageable premises. The once-impressive building, with its façade towards one of the city's busiest approach roads became increasingly forlorn, looking lifeless and empty. The sign 'under offer' had literal and metaphorical connotations simultaneously during the five years it took to sell, the process slowed by problems obtaining permission to redevelop such a prominent grade II listed building.

All has not, fortunately, been lost. Perhaps pig-headed determination, cussedness or contrariness have emerged, in those who never give up. Key figures including remaining staff, community leaders, trustees and, in particular, Martin Dodgson, Murray Holmes and Christine Roche, worked to find a new way forward. They lamented the imminent loss of great experience and knowledge while appreciating the benefits for the future that the past could bring. They found a new building, central and accessible and have been trying to repair damaged relationships and forge new ones.

The parental and patronising ethos that maintained the missioner approach for so many years should never return.

The new centre
in St Mary's
Street, Leeds 9

However, the importance of support for the marginalised and
dependent will never go away. The last century and a half have
taught us that this is at its best and strongest when it is locally
funded and managed, with the involvement of the community
to which an organisation is accountable and responsible.

The constraints of the decade following the financial implosion
of 2008-09 have, if anything, confirmed that short-term
efficiencies come at the disproportionate cost of longer-term
social wellbeing and cohesion. The society has survived all these
changes and returned to its traditional aims, but in a modern
setting. One hundred and sixty years of endeavour have not been
lost, despite all that has happened. The work carries on.

This memoir started as being a very personal account of a
working life. It ends as a testimony of the ethical and political, a
victim of its own circumstances.

Goodbye missioner; hello the future; there is much to learn
from the past. This story of my life is my contribution to the
educational dimension of evolution, warts and all. The lessons
are ones I hope deaf people and those around them will chose
to understand, and fight on.